*Discourses delivered to Swamis and Ananda Samajis of the
Nithyananda Order all over the world*

The meditation techniques included in this book are to be practiced only after personal instructions by an ordained teacher of Life Bliss Foundation (LBF). If some one tries these techniques without prior participation in the meditation programs of LBF, they shall be doing so entirely at their own risk; neither the author nor LBF shall be responsible for the consequences of their actions.

Published by

Life Bliss Foundation

Copyright© 2008

First Edition: May 2008, 1000 copies
Second Edition : October 2008, 2000 copies

ISBN 13: 978-1-60607-005-5   ISBN 10: 1-60607-005-3

All rights reserved. No part of this publication may be reproduced, or stored in a retrieval system, or transmitted by any form or by any means, electronic, mechanical, photocopying, recording or otherwise, without written permission of the publisher. In the event that you use any of the information in this book for yourself, the author and the publisher assume no responsibility for your actions.

All proceeds from the sale of this book go towards supporting charitable activities.

Printed in India by W Q Judge Press, Bangalore. Ph.: +91 80 22211168

Follow Me IN!

Nithyananda

 Published by LIFE BLISS FOUNDATION

Atma Spurana Program, May 2007, Seattle, USA

Contents

PREFACE 9

ALLOW ME! 13
   The Unrealized Knowledge 13
   Work Towards Experience 15
   Let Go of That Identity; Have a Real Vacation! 16
   Revel in the Revelation 18
   Meaning of Atma Spurana and the Koshas 18
   Meaning of Atman – Story from Mahabharata 20
   The Goal of This Program – Making the Self Alive 21
   Meaning of Upanishad – 'Just Sitting' 23
   Sitting with the Master 23
   Beyond Techniques... Do not miss! 24
   The Alchemy 25
   Don't Judge, Just Relax 26
   Dive In! 26
   Mistake Your Identity! 31
   Completely Open ... Listen... 33
   Make Friends ... Just Out of Innocence 35
   Practicing the Upanishad 37
   Be Inside Your Boundary ... Help the Process 39
   Be With Sincerity 43
   The Happening 44
   Owner's Manual for the Mind 46

The Master's Effect on Your TPS 53
TPS and Koshas – the Relationship 54
Questions and Answers 60

ANNAMAYA KOSHA 72
Revisiting Koshas - from a Healing Perspective 72
What is God? 74
The Physical Layer – How You Create It 75
Evolution of Man – Western Versus Vedic Theories 76
A Small Prayer Before We Start 79
Glimpse of an Enlightened Being – What It Can Do 80
Questions and Answers 83
Choosing an Enlightened Physiology 85
Start Now – Clean and Reprogram Yourself! 86
You Are Not Just a Bio-Mechanism;
You Are Consciousness 88
Meditation
- Expel the Animal Engrams 92
Vedic Tradition – Here and Now 94
Relive and Relieve! 96
How You Will Emerge 101
Questions and Answers 104

PRANAMAYA KOSHA 128
Prana and the Five Vital Processes 128
Bring In Awareness 130
Meditation
- Breath Awareness 133
Questions and Answers 137
Auxiliary Simple Humming Meditation 162
'Just Sitting' again... 163
Questions and Answers 164

MANOMAYA KOSHA 196
- Introduction and Meditation 196
- 'Just Sitting' again 199
- Questions and Answers 200

VIGNANAMAYA KOSHA 216
- Koshas and Boundaries 216
- Reside Deeper Within 217
- Awareness Is the Key 218
- Meditation
  - Visualization of expansion 221

ANANDAMAYA KOSHA 226
- What The Masters Say 226
- Our Two Pseudo Identities 227
- The Ancient Tradition Holds The Key 228
- Understanding And Moving Beyond 229
- Preparing To Un-clutch 230
- The Un-clutch Technique 233
- Meditation
  Nithya Dhyaan - Life Bliss Meditation 237

APPENDIX 241

PREFACE

The purpose of man's life is to realize the Self or the *Atman* and merge with Existence. Enlightened Masters have realized this and have devised techniques for others to realize it as well. What is standing in the way of man in realizing this are the five body sheaths called the **koshas**. Man's awareness needs to be pulled through these sheaths in order to reach the *Atman* or Self.

The five **koshas** can be described as below:

- *Annamaya kosha* ('Food body') - This outermost body is made up of the food that we eat. This body represents the tangible physical body that we are all familiar with.

- *Pranamaya kosha* ('Breath body') - This body is responsible for the breath cycle in us that keeps our whole body alive.

- *Manomaya kosha* ('Mental body') - This body represents our mind - our thoughts and emotions.

- *Vignanamaya kosha* ('Intelligence body') - This body represents the subtle or Supreme Intelligence in us which can bring about a deeper sense of consciousness and insight into the inner and outer worlds.

- *Anandamaya kosha* ('Bliss body') - This innermost body represents unconditional joy that can be felt through communion with Existence or God.

Everyone is aware of the 'food body' and most people operate from this layer. Some strive to become aware of the inner body sheaths by practicing various meditation techniques and yoga methods.

The Life Bliss Program Level 3 - Atma Spurana Program (ATSP) is a unique meditation program wherein the five sheaths are discussed in detail and techniques taught to pull our awareness through these sheaths to realize the Self. The *Taitreya Upanishad* forms the basis of this program.

CHAPTER 1

ALLOW ME!

That is Atma Spurana!

I welcome you all with my love and respect.

THE UNREALIZED KNOWLEDGE

First, I wish to tell you a few basic things before we enter into the program:

Whatever knowledge you have with you already, all the intellectual stuff that you have collected till now, from previous programs and from any reading, please keep it aside while you are here. Just sit as an open being. Then, it will be easy for me to help you. It would be a waste of your money if you sat here with all the old knowledge that you have in you already. Any knowledge that you have within you that has not become a solid experience for you as yet, should be sent out of your system. Even if the knowledge was from my earlier programs, if whatever you have heard has not become an experience in you, do not carry it with you. Especially *now*, do not keep it in your head. Whatever has become a solid experience would have left your head long ago. It will be in your being. So whatever is still in the head has not become an experience. So, send it out. Sit in a completely relaxed way. You can be very free and relaxed. When you sit, don't sit with an attitude of 'I know this', 'I know that', 'I have heard this earlier', etc.

Follow Me IN!

A small story:

A young man worked hard and prepared for a presentation, and then delivered it to the target audience. The whole group enjoyed it except one professor – a highly intellectual person. At the end of the presentation, the young man asked that professor, 'Did you enjoy the presentation? What is your opinion of it?'

The professor replied, 'I know every word that you uttered in the presentation. I know the book from which it is taken. Then, how will I enjoy it? Every word which you used is there in that book.'

The young man was shocked and said, 'No, I can't believe this, Professor.'

The professor said, 'I will send you that book tomorrow.'

The next day, the professor sent the book to him. The book was a dictionary!

Understand! You might think that this is amusing, but your mind also plays the same cunning role. It keeps concluding every minute, 'I know everything that he is talking. I read it in that book, I read it in this book, I heard it spoken in that discourse,' and what not. Your mind will always be taking things for granted. Maybe this story is a little exaggerated, but your mind is not far from it. If you watch your mind closely, you will understand what I am saying. You will understand that the basic thread is the same, whether it is your mind or the professor's; just the degree is different, that's all.

Allow Me!

WORK TOWARDS EXPERIENCE

I always tell people: spending years and years in just acquiring knowledge is a mere waste. If you can work towards one solid experience, it is the best thing that can happen to you. What do I mean by experience? Experience means being convinced beyond your logic that ultimate truths are livable, that ultimate truths are reality. That is what I call experience.

Some people who are a little innocent, who don't have a large amount of knowledge stored in them, will have the 'click' or 'experience' easily. Only those who don't want to get rid of their knowledge, those who have vested interests in their knowledge, take ages to experience.

Understand: it is very rare to get the presence of an enlightened Master in your life. I am telling you in very clear words not to miss it. When you are near a Master, you are near such a great *possibility*, so do not waste it, merely because of your mind and the stored information. When I tell this to people, they don't listen, and when I leave the country, they sit and repent for not having fully utilized the time and space around me.

LET GO OF THAT IDENTITY; HAVE A REAL VACATION!

One more important thing: be a little more flowing than your usual self during the time you are here. You are in a safe and blissful zone, so just let go. Don't be frozen and serious. Nobody is here to exploit you; you are in a completely safe and secure zone. So be relaxed and open.

People are constantly holding onto their identity because they feel insecure and threatened that their identity might disappear if they let go. Deep down, all of you have a desire to actually *be* in a place where you don't need to hold onto your identity; where no one will recognize you, and you can just let go and do what you wish to do. So, when I create such a situation, people see the possibility for it to happen, but feel insecure because of that. Just see the self-contradiction!

When you see a beach, or a resort, or a snow covered mountain in a website or on television or in photographs, you always feel that you should be there at that spot, is it not? You visualize and fantasize that you are traveling by boat and enjoying that ambience! But when you actually go to that spot, you don't feel that same joy or ecstasy which you felt when you fantasized. When you think of Miami, it is amazing, but when you live there, it is not so amazing. Why is this so? Because the desire swelling in you, is actually to be in a place where you don't need to hold onto your identity. While this is your real desire, you think that the *place* is the real desire!

You know that there is nobody in Miami who knows you and so you don't have to hold onto your identity for survival. This is the actual thought under all the layers of thoughts. This thought does not even surface consciously; it is there subconsciously. This thought is an expression of your yearning for freedom from identity. This is what you are really searching for, not any fantasy place. Understand this truth very deeply and it will help you to have a real vacation here and now! Your desire for vacation is nothing but the desire to be away from your identity. But when you go there, without knowing the truth that you started out with, you try to establish your identity there also. In two days, you establish your same old identity firmly, and experience the same hell. You settle down comfortably with your old hell.

Now, for these two days, try to have a real vacation. Move away from your identity. First, move away from your friends and family; do not sit next to them. If you sit next to them, you will constantly feel obliged to react the way they would want you to. You will be having some identity or image of yourself with that relative. You will be forced to maintain that identity all the time, if you sit next to them; your words, your laughter, your body language, even the way you sit, etc. You will be unconsciously maintaining it all for their sake. And every time you do that, you will be establishing your old identity again. I have seen husbands who do not laugh completely when they are sitting with their wives. Every time they feel like laughing, they look for some kind of concurrence. If the wife laughs, they will also laugh. So much of bonding is not required! At least, for these two days, you can be a little away from it and relax. It is for your own good that I am saying this, not for anything else.

Revel in the Revelation

Our meditation programs are never designed; they are just revealed. There is a big difference between designing and revelation.

Let us understand this first. This is the first thing which you need to understand. 'Designed' means having prior information as to:

What does the customer want?
What is supposed to be supplied?
How best to package it?
What is the purpose of the product?

'Design' is an analysis of what you want to give, and how you want to market it. With all this information, with all this data, the product is created and marketed.

'Revelation' needs just one thing: the need of the customer, that's all, nothing else. What does the person in front of you need? Then, the Truth, as it should be expressed, simply comes out on its own! That is revelation.

Meaning of *Atma Spurana* and the Koshas

Let us understand the word *Atma Spurana* before entering into the program. Literally when translated, *Atma Spurana* means 'Flowering of the Self'. The word 'Self' needs to be understood. In the Western dictionary, the word 'self' is always understood as 'ego' or 'individual identity'. But in the *Vedic* tradition, 'Self' is not considered as the individual identity. It is the eternally existing Consciousness. *Atma Spurana* is the flowering of this Consciousness.

What are *koshas*?

Koshas literally means 'sheaths' or 'coverings'.

For example, our physical body biologically comprises various systems like nervous system, circulatory system, musculo-skeletal system, respiratory system, etc. This does not mean that these are separate systems each of which has its corresponding body part. The same physical body has a number of organs, a group of which can be classified as performing a certain function. For example, the respiratory system includes all the organs like the heart, lungs, throat, etc which are involved with the functions of inhalation, exhalation and sending oxygen to each and every part of the body and collecting carbon dioxide from every cell of the body.

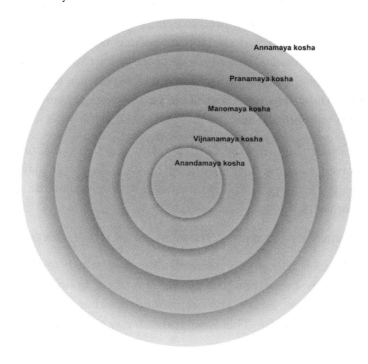

So also, we can classify our body-mind-spirit system in different ways. One such classification is the *koshas*. The *annamaya kosha* is related to the physical body which is the body we can see, touch and feel. The *pranamaya kosha* is related to the breath, which is directly and deeply related to our desires. The *manomaya kosha* is related to our mind and thoughts. The *vijnanamaya kosha* is related to all our feelings and emotions. The *anandamaya kosha* is related to the bliss in us - our true nature.

We don't need to work on the Self itself in order to make this flowering happen. We need to work on something which is *between* us and that Self. Your body, your mind, your emotions, these few things which are *between* you and your Self are what we need to work on. These are called *koshas*; they are energy sheaths, in and around us. Only these *koshas,* which are five in number, need to flower, need to open, need to radiate, need to fall in tune. Understand: the ultimate Self does not need anything; only the *instruments* with which you experience the Self need to flower; they need to open up for you to experience the Self or Truth. All five layers need to be purified so that they constantly radiate enlightenment.

One more thing: in the NSP, we work on the *samskaras* or engraved memories that are printed on the *koshas,* on the layers. Now we are going to work on the *koshas* themselves, on the very canvas itself.

Meaning of *Atman* – Story from Mahabharata

See, in each one of you, there is something which gives you confidence. Even though you die again and again, there is something that gives you a deep confidence that you will not die in the real sense. That is what the *Atman* or the Self is.

Allow Me!

There is a beautiful story in the great Hindu epic *Mahabharata*. It is called *Yakshaprashna:*

There was a demigod named Yaksha who had a quiz program with Yudhishtira – one of the five Pandava princes, known for treading the path of dharma, or righteousness.
The demigod was asking all his questions and one of the questions was, 'What is the most surprising thing on planet Earth?'
Yudhishtira says, 'Every moment, every day, we see so many people going to a mass abode – the abode of death. Even then, every soul, every person who lives here, thinks that he is not going to die! He thinks that he is going to be here forever; that only others are going to die. That is the most surprising thing on planet Earth!'

There is something which gives you confidence; there is some energy that constantly gives you the idea that you are going to be here forever. That is what we call *Atman*! If we understand this truth and catch on to the energy, or Self, behind this thinking, we will celebrate death as a mere passage in the existence of the Self. Instead, if we understand this truth in the context of the *physical body*, we will end up believing that death can never take our body away from us, and we suffer when it actually happens.

THE GOAL OF THIS PROGRAM – MAKING THE SELF ALIVE

Every one of you, every one of us, experiences the Self, but unfortunately, not all the time. Every one of us has got some experience, or at least a vague idea about that Self. Without this hidden belief, there would be no logic for you to hold on to this body. Your holding onto the body is only a disguise of the truth that your Self is eternal. Holding onto this body is possible only because you have some idea, in some corner of your mind, that you won't perish, that you won't die. Consciously you think that it is your body that can't perish, but the deep truth is that it is your Self.

Atma Spurana means flowering of the Self, that Self, that consciousness which is in you; making it alive; making this a solid experience for you throughout your life. The goal, or the purpose of the whole program is making that Self alive, making that a living experience, which will hold good for your entire life.

Making the Self alive was the very goal of the Master/disciple relationship in the *Vedic* tradition. And to achieve this, you should know the significance of these *koshas*. Then, you can achieve inner bliss in a much easier and quicker way. During the *Vedic* times, knowledge of these *koshas* was passed down from the Master to the disciple through the learning of the *Vedic* scriptures such as the *Upanishads*. The *Upanishads* speak extensively about these *koshas*. Knowledge about them was imparted in *Vedic* schools called *Gurukuls*. In the olden days, the disciples went to *Gurukuls* and learned about life engineering, that is, Spirituality. Once they undertook training in such profound truths, the rest of the academics became child's play. The reason is, through *Upanishadic* training, the very learning stemmed from deep consciousness, not from mere intellect.

In *Gurukuls*, whatever be the area of learning for the child, the deep seeking in them for the ultimate truth was continuously nurtured. That was the thread on which everything else was strung. They were continuously prodded to inquire what man's search in life was about. Every human being has this question and the answer for it is deeply embedded in him. It is the responsibility of the enlightened Masters to bring this out of them, and help them achieve fulfilment through it. It is only because this question is not brought out, that we really do not know what we are searching for. The aim of education in the *Gurukuls* was to bring out this question, and to identify the answer.

MEANING OF *UPANISHAD* – 'JUST SITTING'

This whole program is based on *Taitreya Upanishad*. The basic techniques, or the ideas which we are going to practice, are from *Taitreya Upanishad*. The word *Upanishad* is a very powerful word. The translation of that word is just ... 'sitting'... nothing else. Just sitting can do so much in you. Sitting in the presence of the Master, just sitting with the Master, can do so much in you. That is why the essence of all the *Vedic* scriptures is called *Upanishad* or 'just sitting'. It is the ultimate technique.

SITTING WITH THE MASTER

When you sit with the Master, the *Upanishad* ... the sitting ... happens; some strange process starts happening in you, which can neither be called a technique, nor a no-technique. It is literally like cooking, or boiling! By tomorrow evening, you are expected to be completely boiled. In Sanskrit we have a word *Siddha*. *Siddha* has two meanings: 1) enlightened 2) cooked, boiled. So, by tomorrow evening you are expected to be completely boiled or cooked! It is just like adding something to you and taking something away from you, both simultaneously. Whatever can be taken away will be taken away, and whatever needs to be added will be added. The Master's presence is like the cooking fire. Just like in cooking you add some ingredients, remove some ingredients, and in the presence of fire, when you do this, cooking happens. In the same manner when you just sit in the presence of the Master, cooking happens. It is more of a process.

BEYOND TECHNIQUES... DO NOT MISS!

If you have done our first level programs like the Ananda Spurana Program (ASP), Life Bliss Program (LBP), or the Nithyananda Spurana Program (NSP), you would know that all these programs are technique-based. Technique-based means you will be taught some technique in the camp which you can practice here, or you can go back home and practice it. How much effort you put in, that much you will grow. That much will become an experience. It happens.

There are next level programs like the Dhyana Spurana Program (DSP) or Nithyanandam. These are not technique-based. There won't be any technique to practice. Just understanding will be imparted there. The understanding itself will add so much to you. Just the simple, yet deep understanding is enough. It will change your ideas about yourself, the world and the cosmic energy, that is *Jeeva*, *Jagat* and *Ishwara*. If your ideas about these three change, you will be transformed. This is the second level.

Allow Me!

THE ALCHEMY

Now, this program is neither technique-based nor no-technique-based. Technique-based is when you will learn something to be done here and which you can go back home and practice. You will not receive anything like that now. You will not receive anything which you can practice at home. No-technique-based is that which is based on just understanding, nothing else. You will not be doing anything. But now, it is not that you are going to keep quiet either. That is why I say that it is neither technique-based, nor no-technique-based. It is called a 'process', or 'alchemy'. Alchemy is a process where a lower or base metal is transformed into a higher metal by adding something to it and removing something from it.

There is a reason why I want to give this detailed introduction to you. The reason is, I don't want any of you to miss the whole aim of this program. Please do not miss a single session. With technique-based programs, if you miss one or two techniques, there's no problem. You will have 80% of the result. With the no-technique-based program, you don't even need to come for the program, just the DVD is enough! Your physical presence is not needed. But now, not only *your* physical presence, *my* physical presence is also needed. Both of us need to sit with each other. That is why this *Upanishad* starts with a beautiful *mantra*. Let us enter into that *mantra* next.

For the next few days, please decide very clearly: you are going to be here for the whole program without missing a single session. People will come and ask, 'Swamiji, I have to go and pick up my kids. Can I go and come back?' In India we do the *Atma Spurana Program* for four days. But you know that in this country, even if God comes, he has to come during the weekend! If he comes on the weekdays, you ask him for his email ID saying you will get back to him! So for at least this weekend, let us be here completely doing the *Upanishad*. Please do not miss even a single session. Just be with the entire flow.

DON'T JUDGE, JUST RELAX

You can be relaxed; there is no need to be serious. Of course, if you are checking me out, then you will be serious, too serious, trying to constantly judge me and what I am doing. But I tell you: don't bother too much, just relax. I am already judged by 1.2 million people around the world. If you are sitting here, waiting and judging, you are going to miss the whole thing. That is the problem. If you are judging, you will be wasting your time.

Judging is not wrong. The preliminary programs like LBP, NSP, Dhyana Spurana Program… all those programs I have created are for the people who are first-timers, who are judging. But this program, the Atma Spurana Program, I have designed more for the people who are really interested in diving deep. The other programs aim at breadth. This program aims at depth. So unfortunately, if you have not done any of the checking out programs, decide not to waste your time any further. If you have already checked out a bit, then you won't have a problem. You will be completely ready to dive in. So now, don't bother much about judging. Just dive deep into your being.

DIVE IN!

One more thing: you will not be able to understand about me unless you dive into the technology that I have created. And unless you have dived and had one experience, you can't judge either. Unless you yourself have one experience, you can't understand whether I had it or not. Only when you have some experience, you can understand. So even if you want to judge me, jump completely inside. Only then will you be able to judge properly. If you are standing outside and judging, then you are a critic, not a seeker.

There are two ways of looking at things. Understand: a positive doubt such as *maybe what he is saying is right* - if you just have that '*maybe*', that's enough. It is a scientist's mind, a beginner's mind. How a scientist approaches a theory, in the same way, but in the beginner's stage. Then there is scope for so much to happen; so much of work can be done. Otherwise, you will be just sitting and wasting *your* time and *my* time.

Even if you are not able to completely throw away your doubts, decide for these two days that you will strongly believe, you will strongly trust, you will strongly work with the Master, that's all. Doubt will completely disappear only when you become enlightened. But now, you can decide that you will put the maximum possible energy in the direction of working *with* the Master.

You have two paths: you can put your energy into working, or into doubting and wasting time. Now, I am asking you to put your energy more towards working. If you are doubting, I need to waste a lot of time in convincing you and proving to you. I have already convinced 12 lakh people around the world, which is around 1.2 million. That is the number of initiated disciples as of now. And for sure, there are at least a few 'more intelligent' people than you in that number! So just relax from the mind.

Why do you think I have to tell you so many things? Why do I have to take so much time in doing this? Because people waste so much time in intellectual jugglery, that's why.

The other day, I went to a devotee's house. I was telling his daughter to do an LBP program. She told me, 'I will do whatever my mom says, but I should be convinced about it.' I wanted to ask her, 'Does that mean that whatever you are doing, you are totally convinced about?' No! The problem is, in other things in life, we are not bothered about logical conviction, but when it comes to spirituality, we are too cautious. I wanted to ask that girl, 'You must be smoking or drinking. Are you logically convinced that it is good for you?' There are so many things that people are not logically convinced about, but they go ahead and do it. But when it comes to spirituality, they get too cautious. They spend a lot of time and energy in just intellectual jugglery. The real reason is, they do not want to enter into reality, that's all! It is a cunning way of postponing reality.

See, you want to claim yourself as spiritual, but you are not ready to transform in order to claim that! So, you just play with the knowledge. Playing with knowledge is a nice way of postponing reality.

I am telling you very clearly: you are spoilt, corrupted with so many unnecessary words and ideas. It is time now to dump all the words and go in for the experience, for the truth. Ramakrishna Paramahamsa says beautifully, 'People go into the mango garden and do a big survey, a big research. They analyse: how many types of mangoes are there? What is the production cost? What is the sales cost? What is the income? How many trees are there? How many branches and how many leaves are

Allow Me!

there? All the statistics are put down. There are some other people who simply go in, pluck a few mangoes, eat them and come out!

We waste too much time in analysis! The whole time is spent on project planning. No work gets done!

Actually, you don't need so much time with me. Only because you are loaded with words, with too much analysis, do you have to sit together with me for two days for anything to happen. I have seen so many people having the experience without going through any technique or program with me.

A beautiful story...

Just the other day, I visited an ailing devotee. She has not done any of our programs, but she has achieved a far deeper state than anyone else. Actually, I went to heal her, to bless her before she passed away. After healing, I turned towards her feet and did namaskar. When I came out, one of my close disciples who had caught my action asked me, 'What is this Swamiji? You did namaskar to her, towards her feet, why? She has not even done any of our programs!' I told him, 'She has not done any of our programs. All she had done was hear about me, and she felt connected! That's all. She has seen me only once.'

I explained further why I did namaskar to her feet.

In Bhagavata Purana (an ancient Hindu epic), there is a beautiful story where Krishna is painting the feet of Radha with mehandi (Indian concoction for decorative coloring of hands and feet). The rishis got jealous seeing this. They asked Krishna, 'What is this? How can you do this to a girl? You may be in love with her, but you are God, so how can you touch the feet of somebody, and that too a girl? This is too much. We can't digest this.'

Actually their ego was hurt, that's all. They fall at Krishna's feet and touch them. Krishna is touching Radha's feet! Hence they feel they are indirectly touching Radha's feet, which they do not want! That is their real problem.

Krishna answers beautifully, 'Understand: purely by her devotion, she is more connected to me than this body is connected to me, so this body is feeling shy and offering its respect to that body, to that person.'

If you understand this one thing, the *Atma Spurana* is done, nothing else is needed!

Krishna says, 'She is more connected to me than this body is connected to me. I feel she is more close to me than this body. That is why this body is touching her feet and offering its devotion and respect!'

This one sentence has got so many truths. The first thing is, it clearly implies that Krishna is beyond his body. That is why He is able to talk of the body in that fashion. The second thing: the feeling of connectedness happens only through deep trust or surrendering or relaxing, as in the case of Radha. Third: when devotion happens in you, you become much more than God! Understand: when devotion happens in you, you become much more than God! That is what you need to understand by this one sentence, by this one statement.

So, I told the same thing to the disciple who questioned me. I felt that the ailing devotee was more connected to me than this body itself because of her simple faith and devotion. A few days later, she left the body so beautifully and gracefully. She was never trained in the ways of intellect or logic in her life.

Allow Me!

People sometimes think that if you are from the West, you will be stuck in logic and if you are from the East, you will be more towards the being. This is not true. I know so many Indians who are so strong in the head and so many Westerners who simply melt when they see me for the first time! It is to do with the quality of your being, not with *where* you took birth.

MISTAKE YOUR IDENTITY!

Anyhow, for these two days, drop your identity. If you are a doctor, think of yourself as an engineer. If you are a lawyer, think of yourself as a doctor. If you are male, think of yourself as female. Just change your identity; relax from your identity for these two days. You don't know the freedom you will experience if you are able to do this! Just for these two days decide, 'There is no need for me to prove my identity to anyone. I am not going to prove my identity to anyone. I am not going to hold onto my identity.' Just for these two days, be a *Paramahamsa*! The word *Paramahamsa* literally means: instead of society calling me mad, I myself say I am mad, so that I am free!

Just look at me! I don't have to follow any one idea. I don't have to follow any one mould. I give you only one guarantee: that I will not hurt you; that's all. After that, I don't have to prove anything to you. I am not even interested in proving any identity to you. That is why I don't even use the word *swami* in my title. This *swami* word is associated with too much identity, too many problems. That is why I never use the word *swami* in my title. *Paramahamsa* means liberated. *You* can also live the life of liberation for these few days.

As long as you are here, try to even avoid talking. If you start talking, you will have to bring back your old identity; you have to talk in the same way; you will be on the same track. So for two days, just relax; do not carry the identity; do not carry your same ideas; just be like a vagabond.

Actually, hippies are the people who are very close to enlightenment; all they need is a little meditation, that's all. They have all the other qualifications for enlightenment. I lived a hippie for nine years, but of course, not with drugs, only with meditation! If you simply remove drugs, and add meditation to hippies, they are enlightened... over! Nothing else needs to be done. Just remove their drugs and add some meditation. For these two days, let you be enlightened hippies! *Paramahamsa* is just an enlightened hippie, nothing else! Hippie *minus* drugs *plus* meditation *equals* enlightenment, that's all!

For these two days, just relax from all identities; relax from feeling compelled to prove your identity; just be completely relaxed. Don't bother about the results. At the end, you will see that so much can happen in you. So much of transformation can happen in you; you will be a new being, a new person when you leave the hall.

This is such a great opportunity to sit, to experience *Upanishad*. Now, you are going to experience *Upanishads*. It is such a great opportunity to experience *Upanishad* from the very source of the *Vedic* tradition; from the very root! So, all you need to do is only one thing: relaxing from your identity. If you don't have one, you are saved; half the job is done. If you have one, then relax from it for the next two days.

COMPLETELY OPEN ... LISTEN...

Now, we will start the first thing - the initiation. Sit with a completely open being. You can even visualize and feel that you are open. Visualize that you are completely open; that you are a flower fully opened, fully blossomed, fully available; that you are totally relaxed. Just listen to these few *mantras* that I am going to chant. I am going to chant *mantras* from the *Upanishad* on which we are going to work.

Close your eyes. Just sit completely open and in silence. The silence always exists ... inside you and outside you. Sit with a completely open being. Make your inner space available and open, for the downloading of this new software that is going to happen now.

Just visualize very clearly that you are opening your body, that you are opening your *prana* - that is the air circulation; that you are opening your mind - that is, your inner chattering; that you are opening all your emotions; that you are opening your very inner space.

These words are powerful words coming to you directly from enlightened beings, now recited again by an enlightened being, towards enlightened beings, that is you all... *from* an enlightened being *through* an enlightened being *to* enlightened beings...

Let your eyes be closed. Be completely open and relaxed.

Follow Me IN!

(Master chants from the Taitreya Upanishad)

Let these words vibrate in you and penetrate your core. Be completely open. The whole process is now getting inscribed into your inner space, so that it can open by itself. It can take care of the process by itself. It is literally like downloading a software. Just allow it. Put your whole energy into opening up. Allow whatever happens to happen.

(Chanting continues and finishes.)

Relax. You may now open your eyes.

Now, you will see that this very downloading itself will do the process. You don't have to worry that you don't understand the meaning of what I have just chanted. In fact, even if you understand the meaning, try to avoid going into what you think the meaning is. In reality, you don't know the meaning. Sanskrit is not just a linguistic language; it is a phonetic language also. You may know the meaning of the words as written in the dictionary – that is the linguistic meaning. But, you will not know the phonetic experience of it, the other layer of it. So just relax, and allow the downloaded software to work on you.

You have the great fortune of sitting with an enlightened being. Enlightened beings are the only living Gods on planet Earth. If I declare this openly, sometimes, people get irritated. Their ego gets hurt. They ask: how can he claim that? Understand one thing very clearly: don't bother whether *I* am God or not; but just by your trusting this statement, just by your believing this statement, you are going to be helped these few days. I have finished solving all *my* problems. By saying that I am

God or that I am not, I am not going to have any problems. Also, by your accepting that I am God, I am not going to gain something out of it. No! If you don't accept also, I am not going to bother about it. By your not accepting it, my personality is not going to be affected in any way! I am not going to lose confidence in myself. Do you understand what I am saying? Whether you accept it, or don't accept it, my confidence in myself is not going to be affected in any way. I have solved my life already! Only thing: if you accept, it will help you; that is the only reason. For the next two days, it will be a big help for you. In making such a statement, I am proposing it more as a technique, as a method, *than* as a fact. You may take it more as a method, to lift you or to transform your consciousness, than as a fact. So, just take it as a method, and work.

Fortunately, enlightened beings are not selected by voting! They just declare themselves, that's all! Whether people vote or not, they don't care. That is the greatness of enlightenment!

MAKE FRIENDS ... JUST OUT OF INNOCENCE

For the next few minutes, you can go around meeting people, without your identity. I am not telling you to introduce yourself to others. No! Remember: you are not the identity which you were carrying earlier. So, I am not asking you to introduce yourself. Don't go around saying, 'I am a doctor, I am a freelance software engineer, I am from this place, and what not.' Try to experiment with the simple technique of making friends without using your identity! Just go around and make twenty friends without using your identity.

You should not use any of the usual things such as your job, your profession, your career, etc. Don't use any of them. Similarly, don't ask any such related questions to the other person either. Don't ask them, 'Where are you from?' Is it possible to make friends without asking any of these questions, with just the face value... just directly trusting the other person? You are here, I am here, let us just directly trust each other! The matter is over! Why do we need our past track record to create friendship?

Introducing yourself with your track record is like saying, 'Alright, here is my track record. You can now trust me. We can be friends!' We don't need such big files. We don't need a credit report to create friends! Showing your track record is like showing your credit report. It is like saying, 'See, I have a good track record. Let us make friends...' No! Just *you* being *here*, or *you* seeing the other person is enough to create friendliness; to radiate warmth; to radiate love; to radiate the feeling of connectedness.

So, just spend around 10 to 15 minutes, and try this new experiment of creating new friends. Don't go to your own family and friends. If you go to them, you will bring back your old identity. Go to people whom you don't know. Meet at least 20 new persons. When you don't carry your identity, you can express yourself in a more innocent way, in a more simple way. Try to express yourself in a new way, and feel connected. Let me see how you are able to connect without using your identity. Let me have some fun! Just go around. No using identity, no visiting cards allowed! This will also make each of you comfortable with the others in the group.

(The group does the exercise.)

Allow Me!

Alright, come and sit down. Again, I see that families are sitting together. Even if I liberate them, they don't want to be liberated! Ramakrishna used to narrate a beautiful story:

A few fisherwomen went to their village to sell fish. After selling the fish in the market, they were returning, but somehow, it was too late to go back to their homes. They could not find any shelter on the way to rest. They managed to find a single house where a florist was living. He had a lot of flowers in his house.

They asked him, 'Can you accommodate us?'

He said, 'Why not? You can very well sleep here tonight and leave tomorrow morning.'

The women lay down and tried to sleep. But they were not able to sleep, however much they tried. Suddenly, one of them realized what the problem was. The fragrance of the flowers was too much for them. These women were habituated only to the smell of fish! That was the problem. They were unable to sleep amidst the fragrance of the flowers. One of them went out, brought their empty fish baskets, sprinkled a little water on them, put them near their heads and soon, they were all fast asleep!

In the same way, these people cannot live without the old smell of their friends...the fish smell... that is the problem. I tell you: it will be a big liberation for you. You don't have to maintain so many standards. You have so many standards constantly nagging you.

PRACTICING THE UPANISHAD

As I told you, this program has nothing to do with any technique or no-technique. It is a clear process. After this program, you are not expected to practice anything at home. You will not carry back any technique from here and practice it. No! It is a process that we are doing now, and you will carry back only the experience. That will itself do its work. So, just carry the experience that will become part of you.

Before entering into the *Upanishad* - that is the process, let us learn the *Upanishad*. What do I mean by *Upanishad*? '**Just sitting**', that's all. *Upanishad* means 'sit'. You may think, 'I am sitting already!' No. You are not sitting. You are only *trying* to sit. You are not 'just sitting'. Now, you will 'just sit'. Please do not ask questions like, 'How long, why, what are we going to gain, and what not…' I am not going to answer even if you ask these questions. **Just sit**, that's all. Let us see what happens if we just sit. Many things might surface: maybe boredom, or the thought that you came all this way just to do this…' Whatever your mind may tell … **just sit**. Don't listen to your mind. It may tell you anything, but you just sit. No technique, no visualization, no *mantra*, no meditation, not even un-clutching from the mind, no technique needs to be done…do not do anything. **Just sit**. You can tie your eye bands.

Remember only one thing: you are sitting in the presence of a Master. *Upanishad* is happening. **Just sit**.

(A few minutes pass)

Om Nithyanandam….Relax. You can open your eyes.

You might wonder why I am giving you such an extensive preparation. In this Atma Spurana program, the preparation is very important. If you internalize the preparation, you are done with the purpose of the program! That is why I am stressing these points so much. These points are the real truth of this program.

BE INSIDE YOUR BOUNDARY ... HELP THE PROCESS

Upanishad...it is a very powerful process. I request you not to miss even a single session. Next thing, for *Upanishad* to happen, you need to be 'here and now'. It means two things: 1.) You can't sleep as you do normally 2.) You need to be inside your boundary. What do I mean by 'being inside your boundary'? Currently, your bodies are not like your homes; they are more like hotels, like lodges. You put your luggage in it and start roaming around. That is the way you use your body. If you are physically at home, your mind will be in the office. If you are physically in the office, your mind might be planning a vacation. If you are eating, your mind will be watching television. You are never inside your boundary! But for these two days, you are expected to be at home inside your body ... and no sleeping!

There is a small story. I always love to tell this story because I really enjoy this story!

A great preacher, a man who was preaching in the name of God all over the world died one day. On the same day, a rash taxi driver, maybe from Chennai, or New York or Calcutta...Calcutta is number 1, maybe Chennai gets number 2, then New York...Anyhow, a taxi driver died at the same time as the preacher, and reached Lord Yama's court. Yama is the Lord of Death.

Yama did the regular enquiry. First the taxi driver came, as usual – fast! Yama asked, 'What were you doing for a living?' 'I was driving a taxi,' he replied. Then Yama saw the list of sins and merits. Now of course, they must have computerized these lists! He saw the whole list and said, 'Alright, have the golden key and go to heaven.'

Follow Me IN!

Next, the preacher came. Yama asked, 'What were you doing? What's your name?' The preacher replied, 'I was spreading the Lord's name all over planet Earth.' He started giving his regular sermon, as usual - his fully well memorized speech. Yama said, 'Stop, stop, stop. Relax.' Then he saw the list of sins and merits and said, 'I think you need to go to hell.'

The moment the preacher heard this, he started shouting, 'What? Just to a taxi driver, you gave heaven. How dare you send me to hell? I will sue you.' Preachers are professional shouters.

Yama said, 'Relax. Let me explain to you. Here, up in heaven, we are not bothered about what you do. We bother only about the result. This taxi driver, even though he was driving the taxi rashly, was so wild in his driving, that the people sitting inside the taxi and those who were outside on the road, were all the time praying to God for their lives because of him! He made so many people theists. He made them all believers in God. What he did is secondary; by the effect of his actions, he converted many of them into believers in God. But even though you were preaching about God, you were preaching in such a way that you put people to sleep!'

So understand, the problem is: if *you* sleep now, when *I* go up, I will have a problem! So at least, maybe not for your sake, but for *my* sake, don't sleep!

One more thing: if I am telling *Ramayana* or *Mahabharata* or *Bhagavatam*, then you can sleep, because you might have heard these stories earlier, and you may wonder how many times you will listen to the same story. You know the whole story of Ramayana: Rama is the one who will go to the forest, Sita is the one who will be kidnapped, and Hanuman is the one who will go to Lanka. Then Rama will go and kill Ravana. Sita will be brought back, and then the coronation ceremony of Rama will happen. You know the whole story. And how many times will you listen to the same story? Naturally, you will think: for one session, I can take a nap. You can catch up, even if you miss a session. Not much is lost.

I have seen very funny things happening when these stories are staged. In January, we went to the *Kumbha mela* in Allahabad, where I saw these stories being enacted. Not only were the people who were listening sleeping, even the person who was singing on stage was sleeping sometimes!

Anyhow, now I am not going to tell you how Rama lived, or how Krishna lived, or how Christ lived. We are going to directly deal with how *you are living*. So now we can't afford to sleep. Neither can you afford to sleep, nor can I. So both of us have to remain awake. What you will do to keep yourself awake, I don't know.

First thing: no sleeping. Second thing: sitting inside your boundary. This sitting inside your boundary is a very important thing to be understood. Just observe your life. Early morning, when you wake up, when you get out of your bed and start brushing your teeth, your mind is already sitting in the office, thinking about your boss, thinking about the answers that you are supposed to give, thinking about work. By the time you reach your office, your mind is already on the beach, thinking about the beach, or the weekend vacation. If you are on the beach in the evening, your mind is already thinking about when to go back home. The mind will be saying, 'It is cold…and this…and that…' The funny thing about your mind is that when you see beautiful scenery on television, or an advertisement, like a beautiful beach, or a beautiful forest, or a snow covered mountain, you always feel you should be there, and that if you are there, you will be in ecstasy. That is the idea you get, especially with the resort advertisements. And you almost feel that if you are lying in that chair near the swimming pool or on the beach, you will experience heaven! But when you go there, you don't feel the experience the way you had imagined it to be. You don't feel that it is so heavenly. Why? What is happening? Why is it that when we see visually, it seems that we will be in ecstasy, but when we go there, it is not such an experience?

The reason is: the moment you are on the beach, your mind has already started thinking about home. When you are back at home, you have already started thinking about the next day's routine. If your body is here, one thing is sure: *you* are not here! Your mind is not here. That is what I mean by not being inside your boundary.

Now, for these next two days, you will not use your body as a lodge or a hotel. You will use your body as a home. Come back. Just be inside your boundary. Only then I can work with you. You and me, both of us need to sit with each other. You need to be here, only then I can work with you. You need to be inside your boundary. Your skin is supposed to be your boundary at least until you become enlightened. After you get enlightened, whatever life you feel within your skin, the same life you will be felt inside every other skin; inside this pillow, inside this seat, inside everything, you will feel the same life. But, for now, your skin is your boundary.

So come back. Be inside your boundary. Only then the *Upanishad* can happen. Both of us need to sit with each other. That is why this *Upanishad* starts with a beautiful *mantra*, which says: *let both of us not hate each other; let both of us grow together.*

The beauty of education in the *Vedic* tradition is that it is not egocentric. The Master says, 'Let both of us grow.' He is not saying, 'Let you grow, I will teach you.' No! He is saying, 'Let both of us grow.' That is the truth. So, let both of us work with each other. Let both of us not hate each other till we end the process. Let both of us feel connected, at least till tomorrow evening.

BE WITH SINCERITY

Understand: you may sit here like you are attending a weekend workshop or a management course. Any attitude is alright; no problem. But decide that for these two days, you will sit sincerely with the whole process. I am not asking you to accept me as your Guru. Actually, people ask me, 'Swamiji, should I accept you as a Guru?' I say no. If I am your Guru, this question will not arise. As long as this question is there, I am not your Guru; forget about it. Search again. Seek again.

Someone asked me, 'When I accept you as my spiritual Guru, does that mean I have to give up praying to Shirdi Sai Baba, whom I have been worshipping for over fifty years now? I don't feel he is my Guru, but I remember him and pay my respects to him.'

I always tell people, even if you accept me as your Guru, there is nothing wrong in learning from some other source, or Master, or place. Pluck flowers from all the gardens and make a beautiful bouquet for yourself. Nothing is wrong in that. After all, I am here to enrich your life. If somebody else is also enriching it, just absorb whatever comes from them. It's not like a shop where if you come to my shop, I would prefer you not to go to the other shops! Just enrich yourself, wherever you can, or in whatever way you can.

THE HAPPENING

Just for these two days, don't bother about all your internal struggles or unnecessary and useless questions. Just sit with a deeply receptive and prayerful mood inside your boundary. The whole process will happen. The *Upanishad* will start happening. Till tomorrow evening, let us not hate each other. Because I am going to make you do all sorts of things, like for example, your food will be a little delayed, your sleep will be a little delayed, etc. You may face a few discomforts. Do not grumble or grudge. Even if you grumble, I am not going to leave you...! See, the program is fixed. Either you go through with complete acceptance, or you go through with struggle. It is up to you. But you have decided to go through it. If you go through it without struggle, it will be a lot easier for you. So let us not hate each other. Let us feel connected to each other. Let us grow together.

That is the beauty of enlightened Masters. Enlightenment is the ultimate experience, but not final. Understand: the ultimate happening every moment is 'enlightenment'. So every moment, the enlightened being is exploding and growing ... expanding. You may think, 'How can enlightened persons grow?' Maybe 'growing' is not the right word. It is the Ultimate Experience happening every moment. Enlightenment is the ultimate. But it is not that it happens once and it stops. It happens continuously. The right word is 'enlightening', not even 'enlightenment'. It is not a noun. It is a verb! That is the truth. Continuously, the experience is happening. That is why the Master says, 'Let us grow together.' For that, we need simple and honest friendliness. Feeling connected, feeling respect for each other, and taking a conscious decision to work together are all needed. All this is needed at least until tomorrow evening. I am not asking you for your whole life! No! And the important thing is, don't forget to be inside your skin, that's enough. Everything else will start happening.

The Master's presence is very powerful, even if you don't understand it. Whether you understand or not, when you sit around fire, you will have its effect; you will feel the heat. Similarly, whether you understand it or not, when you sit next to the Master, you will see that things start happening inside. Enlightened consciousness is much more powerful than your doubting logic. It can penetrate you. People ask me, 'Should I trust you? Should I believe you?' I say, 'No. There is no need. Your doubt and trust, both are shallow.' Neither is your doubt strong, nor is your trust strong. Both are depending on your mind. But enlightened consciousness is beyond the mind. It can straightaway work on you. Do not bother about whether you have doubt, or trust, or faith, or anything. Sit with a deeply receptive mood and 'the beginner's mind', with a willingness to go through the process. Be inside your skin. That's enough. You will see that the process happens. The *Upanishad* will simply start happening.

Follow Me IN!

Owner's Manual for the Mind

I will just give a simple understanding about how the mind works and how exactly the *Upanishad* is going to help us. Let me once more explain the word *Upanishad*. It means: just sitting. If you want a commentary for that word, I could say: sitting with an enlightened being.

Let us first understand how our mind works with the help of a simple drawing. Your mind is doing nothing but 'making your future into past'. Understand: what you call as life is nothing but swallowing your future and making it into the past. Am I right? The future becoming the past is what you call your mind, or whatever you know as life; nothing else. This diagram is just a time shaft. The space where the future and the past meet is what we call the present moment. The future is just disappearing into the past. Every step of what I am describing, you need to understand completely; only then you will be able to go with it.

A little bit of introduction about the mind is good. It is like an owner's manual. Owner's manual for the mind! We use the mind without reading the owner's manual even once. Even in the car, there is information about the airbag, and it says: for further details, see the owner's manual. How many of us have referred to the owner's manual about the airbag? With airbags, it is alright to ignore the owner's manual, because you may feel it is useful only when you have an accident. But if you don't read the owner's manual for your mind, you will *create* accidents! And you will not even know that you are going through accidents every day. That is the problem. So it's better to have the owner's manual for the mind.

(points to the board)

Allow Me!

This is the present moment where the future is disappearing into the past.

Your mind is nothing but a process in which you constantly jump back and forth between the past and future. If you just observe your mind for a few minutes, you will understand exactly what I am saying. Thought is nothing but jumping from past to future or future to past. Only when you are shunting between the past and the future can you think. In the present moment, you can't think. Try to create a single thought in the present moment. You can't! Either you create a thought *or* be in the present moment. The two are mutually exclusive. The moment you come to the present moment, thoughts will disappear! Thought, and the present moment are mutually exclusive. If thinking is happening, it means that you are jumping from past

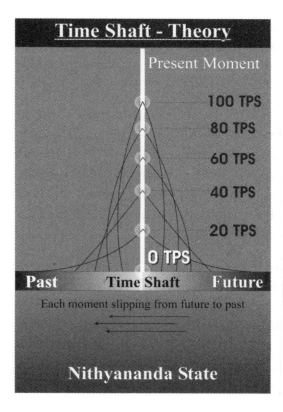

to future or future to past. If you are jumping a 100 times from past to future or future to past in one second, you have 100 thoughts per second or 100 TPS for short. Are you able to grasp what I am saying?

If any of you have any doubts, put it down in writing. At the end of the session, I will answer, because this needs to be completely internalized by you. Understand, only if the internalization happens, you will involve yourself in the whole process.

The problem is, you will do all sorts of illogical and nonsensical things for any pleasure, but even to move *one finger* for spirituality, you will ask one thousand questions. And you think you are very intelligent in doing so. You keep justifying your foolishness by thinking that you are intelligent. That is the problem. Many people come and tell me, 'I know that smoking is bad, but I am not able to drop it. What do I do?'

What do I do? I give them honey. I give them a drop of honey specially energized for de-addiction. Even when your logic says that something is not good, you will do the same thing when it comes to pleasure. But when it comes to meditation or spiritual things, even for a small thing, you will ask so many logical questions. And you think that because your questions are very logical, you are very intelligent. Sometimes, you have the pride, 'I don't believe in superstitious things.' You are dangerously unaware of how many thousands of nonsensical and superstitious things are actually there within you. *You are the body*, is the first superstition that you are carrying! You are not even aware of this! Anyhow, at least now, internalize this, so that you will be ready for the process.

Allow Me!

When you are having 100 thoughts per second (TPS), you will be away from the present moment by that proportionate distance. The present moment is where the future and past meet. If you are jumping too many times, which is what is going on now, naturally you will be away from the present. You will never be in the present moment, because in the present moment, you can't think. There is no space for thoughts in the present moment. If you come back to the present moment, there will only be a beautiful silence. The more number of times you are jumping between the past and the future, the more number of thoughts you will have. 100 TPS means you are completely away from the present moment. You are just not concerned about what is happening in the present. Even if I am standing and talking here, you just pick up one thought, and compare it with all that you have heard in past lectures, discourses, classes, and books, and you remain judgmental about what you are hearing now. You will be sitting and having big comparison notes and missing all my statements. That is the problem. See, I am not saying that whatever you heard is wrong, but sitting and analyzing *at this time* is wrong, because you are missing my continuous flow of statements.

And the problem with so called spiritual seekers is that they are well-read, and completely confused! For any statement that I make, they will be sitting with 10 dictionaries and 10 references and comparing my statement with the statements there. They will be doing two things: either they will refer to all those books, and if they find some relationship with what I am saying, they will say, 'What he is saying is right,' or if they do not find the right quotation or match for my statements, they will say, 'This is not the right thing. I don't think he knows the subject fully. He is too young.' This is the problem!

Follow Me IN!

See: whether you say 'yes' or 'no' to my statements, by comparing notes, you are not going to grasp. Even if you say yes, you are going to miss the other statements which I am making. By the time you finish your analysis and come back I would have gone 10 steps ahead.

So for now, just keep all the things which you have read, or studied or heard, in one corner, for two days. When you go back from here, you can pick it up. I am not asking you to completely throw it away. I am only saying, just for two days, go into my words completely, and understand and internalize. If you are jumping between this and that, you will be away from the present.

Sometimes, because of some meditation that you do, because of some technique that you sincerely practice, you might manage to bring down your TPS to say, 80. This means that instead of moving 100 times between the past and the future in one second, you move 80 times between the past and the future in one second. You come down a little towards the present moment. If you work further and reduce the TPS to 60, you move a little more to the present moment. Sometimes, very rarely, by powerful techniques or by the blessings of an enlightened Guru, you can bring it down to 20. See, these are just indicative values. It is not that you are currently having 100 TPS. You are probably having 1000 or 2000 TPS. Or it may even be a million.

One more important thing...please do not sleep! Sleep does not mean zero TPS! Sometimes...in the silence... people wake up. See, my talking sometimes feels like a lullaby, so you feel relaxed and taken care of. When I give a break, suddenly you

Allow Me!

understand that something is wrong, and you wake up. And the fun part is, when these guys wake up, the first thing that they do is: look at others! If you are looking at others, understand that *you* are the person who slept, not the others! These people who doze off, they will start with, 'Let me listen with closed eyes.' They will have the justification, 'I am meditating and listening'. Soon, the person next to them will see them sitting with closed eyes, and they will nudge them. But these people will not even open their mouth to say, 'I am listening', because then, their sleep will be disturbed! They will say, 'You attend, you listen, I am ok. I am listening.' What to do? I always tell people that 'meditative listeners' are the ones who are thinking about something else, or are lost somewhere else.

Anyhow, coming back to the subject, rarely, in the presence of a Master, or through some process or some initiation, you come down to 20 TPS. When you come to the present moment, suddenly you will have the intelligence to see the future and the past clearly! From a higher TPS point, you can't see the past or the future clearly. When you come down, you may be able to see a little better. The lower your TPS, the better your vision of the past and the future will be. One important thing: now it feels like I am giving you a big promise, but let me tell you: if you come to the present moment, you can *see* your future so clearly!

Let us analyze one important thing. Sometimes, when you are at a party, suddenly you think that some person is going to appear in the next few minutes... some old friend or someone... and you will see that the person is suddenly there! Or sometimes, when the telephone rings, suddenly you will remember someone who was not there in your memory for the past few years. When

Follow Me IN!

you pick up the phone, that person will be on the telephone line! Or when the doorbell rings, suddenly you remember a relative who has not come to your home for the past five years or whom you have forgotten for the past five years. When you open the door, you will see him standing there. How many of you have had these kinds of experiences, at least once or twice in your life? So many of you are raising your hands! But when it happens to you, what do you say? You usually call it a coincidence. If it happens in one person's life once, it can be called a coincidence. Am I right? Practically, 98% of you, say that you have had this experience. When 98% of you have had this experience, how can it be called a coincidence? You can't brush this aside in the name of coincidence. Then you will have to change the meaning of the word 'coincidence'! Coincidence happens rarely, it may or may not happen in one or two person's lives. But now, the evidence says 98% of the people are experiencing it. There is something more than coincidence in this. This is actually what we call 'intuition'. It means, when that doorbell was ringing, or when that cellphone was ringing, maybe due to a sudden jerk or due to some other reason, your TPS suddenly dropped. TPS can be made to drop even by force sometimes. When the TPS dropped, you were able to see the future, maybe the next five minutes of the future clearly. You had a glimpse of the time shaft! That is how you were able to see the person on the other side of the door or phone.

When the TPS drops, you see the future. I think you are able to connect with what I am saying. This is the reason why you will be able to see what is going to come or what is going to happen. See, suddenly, due to the doorbell ringing or the cellphone ringing, or probably because you were really relaxed and happy, maybe because in a party, where you don't have your direct relatives or your in-laws, you were very relaxed...for whatever reason, your TPS suddenly drops. Then, you will have a glimpse of the next five minutes of the future. Just imagine, if your TPS falls, just accidentally, if you can glimpse the future, if your TPS can be consciously brought down, then understand the value, understand the clarity which can be added to you!

Now, the next few statements which I am going to make, are very mystical. Until now, whatever I said looked very logical, and they *are* logical, but the next few statements are going to be mystical.

An enlightened person is the person who is established in the present moment, whose energy is in 0 TPS. He is neither lost in the future nor lost in the past. Understand this. The first statement which I am making is: an enlightened person is the person who is established in the present. It means that if you can bring down your TPS and establish yourself in the present, you are enlightened. Second thing: the future, past and present - all these three put together are called 'eternal.' Eternal means 'nithya'. You can touch eternity only in the present moment!

THE MASTER'S EFFECT ON YOUR TPS

See... eternity can be touched only through the present moment. You can't touch eternity through the future or the past, because both of them do not exist directly under your control, as you think. The past you cannot touch, because it is not there. You can't catch the future also, because it is not there! You can only touch the present moment. You *are* in the present moment. If you want to enter into eternal bliss, or the present moment, or enlightenment, or whatever you want to call it, the only way is to bring down your TPS.

One thing: an enlightened person is a person who is established in the present moment. The next few statements which you need to understand are: if you are in 100 TPS, and you are in the presence of a being who is in 0 TPS, something happens in you. Your time shaft also starts slowing down. This is what I meant when I said that I will be making a few mystical statements. Understand: the person who is in 100 TPS, if he sits with a being who is in 0 TPS, suddenly the TPS drops drastically. Fortunately, the TPS of enlightened persons cannot be raised by you! Only yours can be dropped by them.

TPS AND KOSHAS – THE RELATIONSHIP

Now you need to understand a little deeply. How does the TPS drop?

Let us now understand these *koshas*. *Koshas* are energy sheaths in our system.

The outermost sheath is called the *annamaya kosha* and refers to the physical body that you have.

The *annamaya kosha* is very closely related to the next layer that is the *pranic* layer or *pranamaya kosha*. *Pranic* layer refers to the movement of air, the air circulation that is happening in you all the time. Air circulation is not just inhaling and exhaling. When we come to that layer, I will explain more about it. The third layer is the mental layer or *manomaya kosha*. Your visualization is your fourth layer - *vignanamaya kosha*.

Finally, the fifth layer is the silence or peace or bliss that is within you, which you rarely experience. It is called the *anandamaya kosha*.

Allow Me!

The outermost layer, the *annamaya kosha*, you can think of as the physical layer. You can visualize it as the physical layer. The second layer, the *pranamaya kosha*, visualize it as air. *Prana* is not actually air. It is the *air energy* that is carried by air. Air is simply the medium to carry the energy, that's all. It is the air energy that is required for us to sustain life. The third layer is the *manomaya kosha* – the mental layer. Visualise it as the constant inner chatter that goes on inside you. Inner chatter is your inner or mental layer. The fourth is the *vignanamaya kosha* or the visualization layer. The fifth layer is the *anandamaya kosha* or the bliss layer – the bliss or joy which you rarely experience. Most of the time, you experience only blisters, not bliss! Causeless bliss has become a rare thing in our life.

Understand: we are not disconnected and separate islands as we think. Even though civilization constantly teaches us that we are separate entities, we are not disconnected and individual islands. Maybe in the physical layer, we are all individual islands. For example, if the food is poisoned, only the person who eats it will suffer, not everyone. In this sense, you can think of yourself as an individual. But if the air is poisoned, whoever is breathing will suffer. This means that in the *pranic* layer, in the second layer of our energy bodies, which is to do with our breath, the distance between us is reduced. Going further, if the mind is polluted, a much bigger group will suffer. For example, if one person who is disturbed in the *manomaya kosha*, that is, someone disturbed in the brain, sits as a leader, you know what will result in that entire city. Now, going still further, if one corrupted visualization leads to any action, for example take the visualization of the atomic bomb- corrupted visualization – what happens? It can destroy the entire planet Earth!

Albert Einstein, the famous scientist says, 'I am successful because I did whatever I did by my visualization. I am successful because I can imagine well.' He did not discover the atomic theory, $E=mc^2$ through his logic. He says the formula came first, and after the truth of the formula came out, he developed the logical steps behind it! This means that it was done through visualization. But corrupted visualization can disturb the whole planet Earth. We are all now threatened by this one visualization, by this one invention called the atom bomb. Today, planet Earth has got atomic weapons enough to burn itself 700 times over and over again. Just imagine: burning once is enough, but there are enough weapons to burn planet Earth 700 times! Fortunately, the bliss layer cannot be corrupted since it is in the control of enlightened beings! Otherwise, planet Earth would have perished long ago. Fortunately, the bliss layer key is kept with us. It is not available to the public. That is why planet Earth exists today.

One more thing... this is a mystical prophecy: don't bother much about these things, you will never perish. Global warming and such things will come and go, but it will affect only those people who have created collective negativity. Nothing will happen to planet Earth because this layer is still under the control of enlightened beings. They manage the whole situation!

All you need to understand is that you are not islands as you think. When you come under the influence of a corrupted mental layer, whether you want it or not, you suffer with it, am I right? In the same way, when you come under a person with a pure mental layer, you will see that he is a great leader. Whether you want it or not, you will be touched by all the pleasures and joys created by that person. In the same way, whether you want it or not, when you come in the presence of a bliss layer person, your

Allow Me!

TPS will come down. That is what is meant by *Upanishad*. Sitting with an enlightened person, brings your TPS down.

Because the person has gone beyond the mind, he has entered the bliss layer. As long as you have the mind, you will be disturbed. When you enter the bliss layer, the person has no mind to get disturbed! Rivers can dry up, but the ocean cannot dry up. An enlightened being has become the ocean. In his case, the river has entered the ocean. That is why, instead of others affecting him, *he* affects everybody! *He* influences everybody. The person who affects everybody (positively of course) is an enlightened being. Anyone who comes into his presence gets affected in a positive way, but *he* remains the same. He is not affected by anyone. As the *Bhagavad Gita* says, this person is established in the Self.

The TPS comes down when you sit with the Master. You might ask, 'Then let us sit for half an hour and go back. Why 2 days, unnecessarily?'

The problem is, you have forgotten how to just sit. I have to teach you for 2 days how to just sit! If I tell you to just sit, you will do some sacred syllable repetition or you will sleep or you start praying or you will just become restless. You don't know how to sit with no *mantra* repetition, no technique, nothing... just sitting... You have forgotten the art of just sitting. In Zen they call it *Zazen* - just sitting. You have forgotten that. Just sitting is no longer part of your being. To teach the 'just sitting', it takes 2 days for me, because you know everything except just sitting, except just being. That is why I have to work 2 days to bring your TPS as far down as possible. For example, when you have 100 TPS, you are in the physical layer. When you have 80 TPS, you are in the *pranic* layer. When you have 60 TPS, you are in the mental layer. As your TPS comes down, you go deeper and deeper into the inner layers. When the TPS is completely down, you enter the *anandamaya kosha* – the bliss layer.

Now you are going to sit with the Master in every layer. We are trying to reduce the TPS to bring the frequency of thoughts down. The whole process which we are going to do for the next 2 days is sitting with a '0 TPS being' so that *our* TPS can drop drastically. One more step you can do is, balance yourself to come down to a low TPS in order to sit with him, since you have forgotten how to just sit. You will be consciously balancing yourself so that your TPS falls. We are going to do something just to stop you from doing something else. This doing is what I call 'process'.

You can write questions about this subject alone.

The moment I tell you to ask questions, you will ask about *vaastu shastra*, astrology and what not. Please do not ask questions such as whether *vaastu shastra* is true, astrology is true, will this stone work for me, etc. If a stone can change your life, then you are nothing more than a stone! So ask questions only on the science that I have spoken now. All other FAQs, I will answer in the evening or tomorrow.

Understand, when I say figures such as 100 TPS and 80 TPS, I am saying them only for you to understand the concept. Don't start thinking: I think I am between 61-80 TPS and so I am probably stuck in such and such a layer...no! These kinds of analysis are for professional seekers who seek all their lives without getting even one glimpse of the truth. Some people make seeking their part-time, if not full-time profession. The whole day they will go around and find some stone, some pendulum or some crystal and experiment with it. They will say, 'Oh! This is radiating energy, I could feel the energy,' etc. Sometimes, even *I* will not be able to feel the energy, but just to keep them happy, I say, 'Alright, take it and go.'

Energy is the experience that happens inside you, not anything that happens through a stone or a pendulum. So many books and theories are being sold today on energy play. One thing I have understood: anything highly impractical that you write, sells! I can give you three tips to become a big philosopher and author of bestsellers. First: write what you yourself cannot practice! Second: just keep on talking only about the problem in different ways. Third and most important thing: never give a solution! If you follow these three things, you can become a great philosopher and an author in just 30 days. The problem is, you don't need enlightenment to teach professional seekers; if you are a philosopher, it is enough. For the fortunate ones who have been brought up in a spiritual environment, truths are engraved in their inner space.

Understand: unless you have walked the path, do not talk. Unless you know it completely, its side-effects, after-effects, everything… do not talk. Unless the person is enlightened, it is considered as the worst conspiracy against humanity to teach. In India, if you are still a seeker, a wanderer, there is a beautiful tradition where you are taken care of by the public. You are not forced to take care of your own survival. You are given food, shelter and respect anywhere you travel within India. But remember, the seeking should not be just an outward profession. It should stem from a deep thirst, an urgency to know the truth.

QUESTIONS AND ANSWERS

(Questions to do with TPS have been grouped together for convenience)

Q: Sometimes, what we see in our dreams turns out to be true the following day. Is it because of 0 TPS?

A: No, it is not because of 0 TPS. In the dream, you pass through the *vignanamaya kosha* to *anandamaya*, that is, from the 4th to the 5th layer. The space between the 4th and the 5th layer is where you fall asleep - deep sleep. When you pass through, you pick up one or two rare truths from *vignanamaya kosha*. *Vignanamaya kosha* is where you dream. You pick up one or two things from here. That is all. It has nothing to do with 0 TPS. What happens during the waking state is 0 TPS. If you see your future in the waking state, it is 0 TPS. In the dream state, it is not 0 TPS. It is just an accident.

Q: You said that the TPS is reduced by sitting in the presence of an enlightened Master. You are here now. We are able to sit quietly with reduced TPS. But apart from this, is there any other way to reduce TPS in day-to-day life?

A: Nithya Dhyaan is a meditation technique that will create the Master's presence for you. That is the meditation I prescribe to bring your TPS down. It is an everyday meditation technique. All our ashramites do it everyday in the ashram as the first thing in the morning.

Q: There have been many times during the past two years, when I have thought that I have experienced the near zero TPS expansiveness – bliss or spaciousness. But the mind, the identity, always comes back. How does one become fully established in the 0 TPS state without returning to the mind or ego or identity?

A: Getting established is a thing achieved by practice / *sadhana*.

Q: Do artists have high TPS or low TPS?

A: They have low TPS; maybe 20 or 40 TPS.

Q: I understand that I can have 0 TPS only in your presence, or when I get enlightened. Am I right?

A: In the Master's presence, 0 TPS will start happening. When you get enlightened, it will still be there. I can give you a glimpse of 0 TPS. If you choose to stay there, you will get enlightened. When you become enlightened, you will stay in the same state forever.

Q: Is 0 TPS, a state we always need to stay in? If yes, then how does one do the day-to-day activities, job etc.?

A: In the real 0 TPS state, you will be most productive! That is the truth. You will be highly productive because you are not wasting energy in unnecessary jumping between past and future. Your decisions will be very sharp. 0 TPS is the high energy zone; you will never become mentally fatigued. You will never say, 'I am done.' You will be so joyful. You will become more productive in whatever you are doing.

Productivity is never disturbed by the 0 TPS state. To tell you the truth, you guys do not spend time on showing productivity. You spend time only on selling yourself. What do I mean by 'selling yourself'? You sit and spend all your time on project plans, deadlines, projections and fooling the bosses. When you are in the 0 TPS state, you will excel just out of your 'quality', not out of your 'marketing ability'. When you excel out of 'quality', you will feel so fulfilled. *Dharma* or righteousness always gives fulfillment. The person who can sell himself can get into politics or a high posting in an organization, but he will never have fulfillment. The person who is *dharmic*, is the one who will be productive and fulfilled. He will attain levels out of his own quality, not out of his marketing. Excelling without selling yourself always gives fulfillment. Put your energy more on *being*; you will see that you become more productive. Apart from just becoming more productive, you will feel deeply fulfilled in your personal life. You will start living a beautiful life. A real 0 TPS person will be *dharmic and productive.*

Q: If I meditate with another person who also meditates regularly, both of us get to a higher state. If I meditate with a restless person, will my TPS become higher?

A: Group meditation will always cause low TPS. And especially in our *satsangs*... I have given a promise that wherever our people gather to meditate, I will be there. If people gather and dance, I will be dancing in their midst, in spirit. When they gather to talk about my teachings, I will be there. So group meditation will always bring down your TPS.

Allow Me!

Q: If every teacher and student both become changed through interactions, how is it that the TPS is not increased for an enlightened Master?

A: This is a nice question! Understand: when an enlightened Master or *rishi* says, 'Let both of us grow together,' it does not really mean, 'I am going to grow by you.' It just shows their humbleness, their openness. It does not mean: I am going to learn from you. It just shows the humbleness. So, just be relaxed. You see: when I do *namaskar* to you, I am not coming down to your level. Instead I am bringing you up to my level! Understand this clearly every time you see me doing *namaskar*.

One day, Ramakrishna Paramahamsa, an enlightened master was doing Kali puja to Sharada Devi whom he later married. The puja was the same that he generally performed to the Goddess Kali. Sharada Devi was a young girl at that time, and was living just like any other girl of her age. She had not yet attained enlightenment.

One of the disciples asked her, 'Mother, Gurudeva did puja to you. Don't you think that he has come down one step by doing so?'

Sharada Devi's reply to this question made people become aware of the level of her maturity and understanding, and why Ramakrishna did puja to her.

She replied, 'He did not come down one step, but instead, he helped me step up by one plane in spirituality. From this moment onwards, my responsibilities have increased.'

If someone accords you a similar respect, what will you do? You will not stand on your feet. You will start flying in the air!

Once in India, when I was entering the meditation hall with my palms joined in *namaskar*, an elderly man was standing there, and instead of doing *namaskar*, he simply blessed me! The person who was standing next to him asked him, 'Why are you blessing, when Swamiji is doing *namaskar*?' He said, 'After all he is a young person, younger than me; I can bless him.' I told him, 'When I do *namaskar*, I do not come down to your level. Instead, I bring you up to my level.' When Masters say that, they show their humbleness, their openness and respect for you. If I have to learn from you, you will project yourself onto me! That can never happen, don't worry!

Q: People treat you as God, and people worship you as God. How do you feel Master?

A: Firstly, I do not have a mind to feel anything! In the way you enjoy seeing my form, I also enjoy seeing my own form. Now, I am sitting on the throne. I can get down anytime from this throne, whenever I feel like, is it not? Similarly, I may also go out of this body anytime I feel like, and then come back to it!

Look at this handkerchief in my hand. There is a small thread hanging from one of the sides. Although the thread is a part of the handkerchief, it cannot be the handkerchief itself. The Master's body is like the thread whereas he himself is the all-pervading energy. Once a person becomes enlightened, the body is only the thread.

Understand: the power of the Cosmic Nithyananda is what drives the body of the six-foot Nithyananda. What does Cosmic Nithyananda mean? The true state of Nithyananda is Cosmic Nithyananda - it is like the whole handkerchief. The thread which hangs from the kerchief is the six-foot body of Nithyananda. The decisions of the Cosmic Nithyananda control this six-foot body.

As soon as enlightenment happens, there is no separate thought, action or decision of one's own. The *annamaya kosha* is transformed completely during enlightenment. It becomes completely blissful like the *anandamaya kosha*! Ramakrishna says, 'For the modern day man, just looking at the Guru's image itself is a great meditation technique.' Just looking at the blissful image of the Guru can lead you to enlightenment.

Q: Your great words are so assuring. I feel connected and in bliss. Does it mean that I am thinking of the past and living in the present?

A: You are living in the present. Bliss can never be felt based on the past. Bliss is always to do with the moment.

Q: How can I prepare myself psychologically for enlightenment?

A: Psychologically, preparation has no significance in enlightenment. Enlightenment is actually blasting you every moment. Whether you have one candle in the house or not, it will not make any difference to the sun. Your psychological preparation is like having one candle to welcome the sun. It will help only till I blast you! After that it won't matter whether you have the candle or not. The psychological preparation is not going to make a big difference. Don't bother about it.

Follow Me IN!

Q: Does enlightenment seem far because of my own fear?

A: Yes, your own fear is the only problem. Don't bother. Just relax and sit here. If you relax with trust, everything will be taken care of.

Q: On the same day that ATSP ends, I am visiting relatives in the evening. They will ask many questions. I am sure that I will not feel like answering them. What should I do? How do we keep quiet, even when social pressure is on us to respond?

A: Normally, these kinds of problems are more prominent in Indian society! Of course, in the Western world also, it is there mildly these days.

Just don't talk to them, that's all. What is there in it? What are relatives, really? Each one is an individual. 'Relatives' is nothing but a badge that you give them. Each one is an individual, traveling the path alone. You need not disrespect anybody, but you are also not answerable to them in such matters. It is your own personal matter. No one but the Master can help you in this matter. When it comes to spiritual life, Ramakrishna Paramahamsa says that anything can be sacrificed. He goes to the extent of saying that even your wife or husband can be sacrificed; even father or mother can be disobeyed.

In the journey of enlightenment, let me tell you one incident that happened in Ramakrishna's life:

One of Ramakrishna's young and very close disciples called Rakhal or Swami Brahmananda, was married at the age of 14 before meeting Ramakrishna. He had a child too. It was a custom in Bengal to marry at a very young age.

Allow Me!

Of course, after meeting Ramakrishna, he felt that his parents had made a big mistake by getting him married at the age of 14. He felt very bad that he could not tread the path of sannyas.

He went to Ramakrishna and said, 'I want to get initiated into sannyas very badly. My wife is not allowing me to. She is forcing me to live the worldly life. There is constant argument and grief happening. Somehow, I am not able to digest the whole thing.

Ramakrishna said, 'Go and pray to Mother Kali.' The man prayed. There is a small ritual of offering betel leaves and betel nuts to Mother Kali and then throwing it into the sacred Ganges river. The man performed this ritual.

Eight days after that, the wife died!

Please do not think anything negative about this story at this point. Let me continue...

When the disciple came and conveyed this to Ramakrishna, Ramakrishna said, 'You are born for sannyas. She came just to finish some of her karma. Her karma is over, so she has left the body. I did not kill her.'

He did not kill her. You have to understand this very deeply. You can very easily think that Ramakrishna used some supernatural powers and planned her death. Just understand: things happened according to the laws of Existence.

Ramakrishna finally told the man, 'You take sannyas,' and he initiated him into sannyas.

One more very surprising thing: after sometime the son also died! The son probably died after 10 to 20 years, but the wife died just 8 days after the ritual!

Q: When I do a meditation, I start feeling different within me. I feel anxious and afraid.

A: Don't bother. It is just an initial level feeling. It will go away. When you start meditating, you will feel yourself dissolving. You will feel as though your identity is dissolving. So, you start to feel afraid. Just allow the dissolving to happen. That is the whole idea. The very idea of meditation is to lose your solid identity and merge with the Whole.

Q: Are you the 'Mother Kali' avatar?

A: Don't bother about whether I am an avatar or not. You have to realize that you are an avatar! That is my mission. My mission is not to prove my divinity. My mission is to prove your divinity.

Q: Is there a correspondence between chakras *and* koshas*?*

A: No, there is no correspondence. Let us keep the discussion on *koshas*, only.

Q: If, to be in the present implies 'not thinking', then how could a scientist or wise man take decisions and still live in the present moment?

A: Whatever they discovered, they did in the present moment, without any thought. It was a sudden revelation. The revelation itself happened in one moment, in the present moment, not based on the past or the future. The rest is logical analysis.

Allow Me!

Q: Sometimes we have a bad dream. Does that mean that the vignanamaya kosha is corrupted?

A: Yes.

Q: Is eternity what is being in the present moment?

A: Yes, if you are in the present moment, you are in eternity.

Q: How do you stay in the eternal present, and deal with the future or past for working sake, as you do?

A: I do not work with past and future. When you actually establish yourself in the present moment, you can just stop and see the past and future as you wish to. Time shaft is like a video game. You can rewind or fast-forward!

Q: If some older people are going to speak of good and bad experience again and again, and not accept the present, how will it affect the younger generation on which they force it down?

A: I think you are talking about in-laws or grandparents! Somehow, when the present is not enjoyable for them, they are caught in the past, in the good and bad of the past. So they will catch you, and start telling you stories: in 1963, when I was in the army....etc! And sometimes, they will tell the same stories everyday. They forget that children have good memory! Not only that, sometimes people listen to them because they will get candy from them at the end of it. What do I mean by candy?

Money... wealth! With me, just because I don't shout at them, they tell me also these stories! Even if I tell them that I know the story, they will insist on finishing the same old stories again and again. They will not even be creative and tell new stories.

You have to know how to handle it. They will not handle it. Nothing much can be done about it. Just be ready to sacrifice the candy that you get in the end, that's all. As long as you want the candy, you have a vested interest in their stories, so you have to suffer. If you are ready to renounce the candy, you will not even ask this question. You will simply handle it yourself, and be relieved. In most cases in India, the older generation hold properties. Unless you listen to their stories and humour them, you can't get the property at the end of the game! So until they die, you will be putting up with them. Sometimes, relatives even pray for their death! If you are a girl, when you get married and leave, you will get a portion of the wealth, like jewels, etc. If you are a boy, you have to please them in some way or the other all the time, so that you are assured of your share of the property!.

Q: Why do we bounce back into the mental and physical layers soon? Why can't we go deeper and experience bliss completely?

A: *I* should ask *you* this question! When you can have a glimpse, why can't you stay there? It is because *you* want to come back, that you are coming back! Maybe your *samskaras*, that is your engraved memories, are bringing you back again and again.

Chapter 2
ANNAMAYA KOSHA
The Physical Layer Created from Memories

Revisiting Koshas - from a Healing Perspective

The allopathic system of medicine is related to the *annamaya kosha*, the physical layer. For all problems related to *annamaya kosha*, allopathic medicine is the best cure. Allopathic treatment plays an amazing role in all sorts of problems related to *annamaya kosha*. Injuries caused in accidents occur in the *annamaya kosha*. Intensive care, emergency care, etc are available in the treatment of *annamaya kosha*. It is only allopathic remedies which are useful for treating fractures and other injuries related to accidents.

The trouble starts when the layers beneath the *annamaya kosha* need to be treated. After trial and error with various medicines, people realised that close to 90% of illnesses were psychosomatic in nature, and it came to be accepted that allopathic medicine was not very effective for it.

Today, research on mind-body medicine is happening at a very fast pace in the world of medicine. People have begun to explore the deeper, subtle layers that are inside the physical body.

Annamaya Kosha

Research is being conducted on the *manomaya kosha*, looking deep inside the physical body, the *annamaya kosha*.

The physical body, which we think of as solid, is not solid at all. It is like this: The Cosmic energy is all-pervading. The various living forms, such as trees, animals and the human body, are actually different forms of the same energy.

How is it that this cosmic energy is available in various forms, yet remains one?

Let us understand this with an example.

Suppose you have a picture of a wave that is six to twelve feet high. Is this wave a truth? No! It had just risen, when the picture was taken. The next second, it would have fallen. But how huge it looked when it was at its peak! But the very next second, the same wave ceased to exist. Only in the picture, the wave seems like an independent object. Apart from the photograph, the wave would be part of a continuous motion.

Similarly, we see various objects only through the mind. We are able to see objects independently only due to the presence of our mind. If we did not have the mind, we would not be able to realise the boundary between our own body and that of a chair that is present in front of us. Everything would be seen as a whole.

People who have slipped into deep meditation say that suddenly they feel they have totally lost their self. This is because the mind becomes still. This is the case of man going beyond the mind. This is the experience when you go beyond the *manomaya kosha*.

One more thing: Allopathy can cure the problems that affect the outermost layer of the human body. A person has to go for allopathic remedy to fix a broken bone. However, after it has been plastered, for the actual healing to happen, the energy play has to be addressed, nurtured.

There is a popular quote amongst the doctors: 'Doctor Stitches, God Heals!'

What is God?

God is the all-pervading, pure form of energy. God is neither an individual nor a character as we think. If we are able to connect to this pure form of energy, then we can maintain eternal youth. The energy called God is available aplenty in every single layer of our body. However, it gets filtered as it passes through each of the layers.

The divine energy is overflowing in the deepest *kosha*, which is the a*nandamaya kosha*. It is reduced in the v*ignanamaya kosha* and gets lesser and lesser as it comes towards the outer layer.

The medical system suitable for *Annamaya Kosha* is Allopathy.

The medical system suitable for *Pranamaya Kosha* is *Yogasana* and *Pranayama*.

The medical system suitable for *Manonmaya Kosha* is Homoeopathy.

The medical system suitable for *Vignanamaya Kosha* is Nature Cure and *Ayurveda*.

The medical system suitable for *Anandamaya Kosha* is Energy Healing like our Nithya Spiritual Healing.

Only the healing touch of the Master or the healing energy passed through divine meditation, can heal the problems related to *anandamaya kosha*.

The Physical Layer – How You Create It

So, please sit up with your spine straight in line with your neck and head. We will start the process on the first layer. Let us now work on the first layer that is the *annamaya kosha*. The layer that is the physical layer - the body which you are carrying now, the body made of flesh and bones and blood.

Annamaya kosha is the material part of Creation. Whether it is a tree or a rock or man, all these have the *annamaya kosha* in addition to having different degrees of consciousness. This *kosha* is the gross manifestation of energy as matter, in different proportions and strengths. It is the first layer of skin, muscle tissue, bones and organs. It is called the gross body, the tangible part of yourself that you can mostly see, touch, and feel.

You have actually created this body of yours out of so many engrams, or *samskaras*, or engraved memories, belonging to past lives. The base material out of which you created this body is your engraved memories or *samskaras*. Engraved memory means the memory out of which you do all the actions, including your thinking. The engraved memories or *samskaras* are the base material out of which you have created this body. If you ask me whether I believe in a person having many births, I don't just believe, I know it is the truth. You go through many births. The *samskaras* which you collect in the many different births - out of *that* you create your body for this birth.

Two things you need to understand: all *samskaras* or engrams will have a certain power, a certain energy in them. There will be an energy and a certain love or hatred attached to it. Let me describe this engram concept very clearly so that you will understand what I am trying to convey. Let us take some engram: for example the engram to have a cup of coffee as soon as you get up in the morning. When you get up in the morning, you will have that urge to get up, go to the kitchen, pick up the coffee and drink. The picture of coffee and the experience of coffee - both these put together is what is called *samskara*. Now, we are trying to remove the picture and give the energy alone to you. If you remove the engraved memory completely, you will lose both the energy and the picture. But when you work on the *annamaya kosha*, the memory's energy will be there, but the pictures will disappear! The *vasanas* will be removed but the *shakti* or the power of the *samskara* will stay with you. *Vasana* refers to the object that created the *samskara* in the first place. It is like the seed. *Shakti* is the power of the *samskara*. Removing *vasana* but not the power of the *samskara*, is called Self-actualization. Understand: Self-realization can be achieved in two ways: by completely removing the *samskara and* the energy. This is the path of renunciation; or, by having the energy but not the *vasana*. This is the path of self-actualization.

Now, by working on the *anandamaya kosha*, you will be having the power but not the pictures.

Evolution of Man – Western Versus *Vedic* Theories

The *Vedic* way of putting the theory of evolution is the most beautiful way. Understand: Charles Darwin missed an important point in the theory of evolution. If Darwin had caught a little bit of the energy of enlightenment, the whole history of the West might have been different! He took the monkey as the father figure; there lies the problem! The *Vedic* tradition says, man came down from God! Darwin says, man came down from the monkey! The throne is given to God in one tradition and to the monkey in another tradition. Whoever you put on the throne - you will remember and live like them. That is why Darwin missed the game. He did not catch the exact thread.

Again, Sigmund Freud, after 40 years of research, concluded that human beings, as such, can't be helped or healed! After 40 years of research, he said this. The problem is, he did not get a single enlightened specimen to work with! He worked only with patients, with sick people, who had not experienced the flowering of enlightenment and hence the totality of being a human. So, he was led to conclude that that was the normal state. He concluded that man, as such, was sick, and hence can never be helped or healed!

A follower of Sigmund Freud went to Tiruvannamalai, a spiritual nerve-center in South India, and my native place. He was afraid to meet enlightened Master Ramana Maharishi and so came away without meeting Him. He writes, 'I was afraid I would be lost in His presence. I have done too much research, and I have too much investment in my beliefs. All my beliefs might disappear if I meet Him and sit in His presence.' Just see his mind game! It clearly shows that he was not a true scientist! He was just a marketing person; one who sells himself, not one who works for the truth. Understand: if you are a scientist, and you sign an agreement with a company, you are completely bound. The moment you sign an agreement, you give up your freedom to research the real truth. Then, you are no more a scientist. You are not a true seeker. In the same way, this man had lost the truth. In olden days in India, there was a taxi which you had to push half the distance and the other half, it would go by itself! This man writes in his reminiscences, 'Such a taxi came to take me to Ramana Maharishi's place. That morning, some fear gripped me and I simply took the taxi and ran away to Chennai. From there, I came back.' He went all the way and was just half an hour's distance away from Ramana. If he had met *Bhagwan,* the whole Western analysis of human psychology might have been different. They would have enjoyed the science of enlightenment!

You see: these people have done enough research in the waking state, dream state and deep sleep state, but they missed the *samadhi* state! If only they had one enlightened specimen, they would have been flabbergasted by the results! They would have had real fun with science, defying the results recorded!

In the *Vedic* tradition, evolution is linked to the different *avatars* of Vishnu. The first is considered to be the fish body. You are born as a fish. You accumulate some *samskaras* through a few incidents when you are a fish. Then, you see a tortoise going around. You see a better possibility in the body of the tortoise. You decide: next time I create, I will create a body like that. A tortoise can live in water and on land. Then, when you are in the tortoise body, you see a better and bigger body, like that of a pig or some other animal. Then you decide, 'The next time I create a body, I will create that kind of a body.' So when you die, you create the next level - that is the pig body. As this cycle happens, you evolve, and also collect different engrams or *samskaras* every time you take birth anew. You raise the frequency of the system, or the body, every time you are given a chance to create or design. This same sequence, you can see in the incarnations of Lord Vishnu as well! First, it is the *matsya avatar* – the fish incarnation, then the tortoise, then the pig, then half-man, half-animal, then the pigmy man, then the primitive man, then the civilized man like Rama, who is *dharmic*. Lastly, even beyond civilization, there is the civilized *poorna avatar* – the completely enlightened being, who is not bound by any rules and regulations, who is just radiating joy, energy and enlightenment. It is this evolution that happens in man also. Step by step, different kinds of beings happen. At every stage, you collect *samskaras* and design a body, when you are given an option, in a better way. This is the process of the evolution of the physical body, and the intelligence of evolution.

A Small Prayer Before We Start

Anyhow, let us both work together. Let us not hate each other until the process is over. This is a very important thing, so understand and remember this statement deeply. Let us not hate each other till the end of the program. I say this because, when the Master starts doing his work on you, burning all your cancerous points, the points where you have invested your ego, you will experience hatred towards him. Right now, this may seem impossible to you, but when the work starts, you will be surprised!

During these few days, your food will be a little delayed, your sleep will also be a little delayed. Please bear with it. This is required, because if you are caught in your regular routine for these few days, your second and third layer energies can't be awakened. You cannot be brought back to life from your deep sleep. So understand the whole truth, only then will you be able to enter into the process.

GLIMPSE OF AN ENLIGHTENED BEING – WHAT IT CAN DO

Ramakrishna Paramahamsa says of himself, 'Even *seeing* me is like a glimpse of enlightenment for a person!' He used to go to Calcutta in a horse carriage. He lived a very joyful life - picnicking, going out, jumping, dancing, etc. He did not undertake the responsibility of a mission during his lifetime. Ramakrishna Mission was not created by Ramakrishna. He initiated around 60 disciples. When he died, only *they* gathered. He says, 'Even if someone sees me accidentally, they don't even have to understand that I am enlightened. Even if they just see me casually, they are blessed!' You might think: how can that be? It sounds too egoistic. It is like me saying that if my car is standing at the signal and another car comes next to my car, if the person in the other car just happens to turn and look at me, he is blessed! He doesn't have to understand that I am enlightened. He does not even have to think that I am a holy man. Just a casual glimpse is enough! Ramakrishna says he is blessed! How can that be? When you understand how to design your body after death, you will understand this statement.

A small incident from Ramakrishna's life:

> *One day, suddenly, he permitted his photograph to be taken. He selected one of the three photographs and said, 'Please make prints of this photo. This is going to be worshipped by thousands of people.' Ramakrishna kept the print in the prayer room, and worshipped the photograph. The people who saw this were confused by this act of Ramakrishna and asked him the reason.*

Ramakrishna explained that he was in the samadhi state when that picture was taken, and hence it had become the very form of Parashakthi (cosmic energy), which could be worshipped.

Another interesting story from the life of Krishna:

Once, Krishna and Arjuna were walking in the forest, after the Mahabharata war was over. Suddenly, Arjuna said, 'Krishna! You told me so much in the Bhagavad Gita during the war. You delivered such beautiful aphorisms. But because I was feeling deeply troubled at that time, I am unable to remember them all clearly. Can you please repeat it to me now? I will absorb it deeply in my mind.'

Krishna replied casually, 'What? You do not remember! Even I do not remember anything now!'

Arjuna was perplexed. He asked, 'What are you saying Krishna? How is it that you yourself don't remember what you said?'

Krishna replied, 'Yes Arjuna, I would have remembered if I had told you all the sutras myself.'

Now Arjuna was even more perplexed and said, 'Krishna, do not confuse me. It is you who told me the seven hundred verses during the war. If you say that you did not tell me, then who did?'

Krishna replied calmly, 'All that was said was not spoken by me, but by the Parabrahma Krishna – the cosmic Krishna! The Krishna who is talking to you now is Vasudeva Krishna – Vasudeva's son!'

Through these stories, understand that the physical body of enlightened Masters is not their own. Whatever they do with their physical body is only through divinity. They are a pure channel for Existence to flow. That is why getting even a glimpse of them is enough in a lifetime.

Follow Me IN!

Understand: whatever *samskaras* you collect when you are alive, gets recorded in you, even if you have not paid conscious attention while collecting them. For example, let us say that you were driving your car, and on the way, some accident or some loud expression of grief was happening in the road. You did not really observe much; you just drove past quickly. Consciously, you may not have even registered the car number, the color of the clothing of the person, or the face of the person who was involved in the accident. But, if you are hypnotized, you will tell the exact car number, the color of the clothing, the person's face, etc! What does this mean? It means that, even if you don't pay attention to the scenes in your life, there is a system inside you which records anything and everything happening around you! Anything happening around you is getting recorded inside.

When you leave the body, all the things which gets recorded in your entire life will replay in front of you. Like an option, your mind will ask what you want to pick up. See, by natural intelligence, you know that the body of an enlightened being which is there in your memory is the best body to choose. But you choose only out of whatever is available in front of you. When you are living as a fish, if you have seen a tortoise even once, you will choose only a tortoise! From the fish stage, you can only take one jump at a time - like the zoning system in USA! Only one jump at a time. There is nothing else you can do. But the next jump you take, will be based on the best information available, the best data available.

One important thing: the onlooker, the man who got a glimpse of an enlightened being during his previous birth, may not recognize that he is enlightened, but after death, the memory will show him very clearly that he had the *darshan* - glimpse - of an enlightened person. This happens because that memory alone will shine! At the time of death, that will be in multicolour, while everything else will be in black and white!

Yes...any questions till now?

QUESTIONS AND ANSWERS

Q: Some people are born blind or handicapped. Why is that? Did they consciously choose it to be so?

A: Yes. They consciously chose. I was once healing an autistic child in America. The child was born and brought up in a Telugu speaking family. When I put my hand on the child to heal, the child started talking to me in singular Tamil, a child who was 4 years old! He spoke to me, 'Remove your hand.' I slowly asked him, 'Why are you asking me not to heal you? Don't you know that I am here only to heal you?' He replied, 'Yes, but I don't want to get healed. I am the owner of this body. I have consciously decided to take such a body.' I asked him why. He replied, 'I am not interested in taking the responsibility of going to school, going for a job, etc. I hate this civilization. I just want to rest and relax. I don't want anything to do with the so called civilized life. That is why I chose autism.' I told him, 'But your parents are suffering. They are such nice people. They are suffering because of you. Why did you decide to be born to them?' He replied, 'Only because they were nice people, I chose to be born to them! They will take good care of me.' Remember: he was answering all these things logically in Tamil! The whole family was looking baffled and troubled because this boy was talking in Tamil so fluently! Not a single person among them knew Tamil. I don't want to reveal the identity for privacy reasons, but this incident actually happened.

Your birth is your conscious decision, your conscious choice, the reason for which only *you* know. Sometimes, a particular part of the body might have been involved in some activity which you did not like, so you will renounce that part of the body when you take birth the next time. Just because of hatred towards that activity, you renounce that part of the body itself! It is true!

Q: Even if we do the mistake just once, will we renounce that part of the body?

A: If that one instance created a strong memory, then yes, you will renounce it.

You see: when you leave the body, and you are about to choose the next body, all the cards will be in front of you. Naturally, you will pick up only the Master Card. You will say, 'I have played with all other cards like Visa Card, etc....now I want to play only with the Master Card. You would have got tired with all the other types of cards. So you decide, it is time to pick up the Master Card. That is why Ramakrishna says that even *seeing* an enlightened Master casually is a blessing! It *is* a blessing.

Never take an enlightened Master's *darshan* for granted. Working with him or knowing that he is enlightened is secondary. Just understand that *getting a glimpse* is a blessing. The entire planet Earth does not have more than 2000 enlightened Masters. When I say 2000, I am also including all those persons who are claiming that they are enlightened also. If there are 2000 enlightened beings on Earth, what are your chances of meeting one in a single lifetime? Half a million is the maximum number of people you might see in your lifetime. In 6.5 billion population of the world, half a million is about 10%! So understand: you are clearly blessed to be a part of that 10%. Don't take yourself for granted. Don't think that having *darshan* of a Master is a casual thing. Further, in that 10%, probably only 0.1% will work with him – like going to his meditation camps, sitting around him, etc. Even setting your eyes on him for a brief moment, puts you in the 10% category! Just imagine! So don't take yourself for granted. It is a very dangerous attitude. Be very clear: you are blessed.

CHOOSING AN ENLIGHTENED PHYSIOLOGY

When you choose the next body, you will sit and try to recall the best physiological structure that you have seen in your entire life. You will analyze the best physiological structure possible and naturally, the enlightened physiology is the best! Human beings are the best physiological structures as of now. And naturally, out of whatever human structures you collected in your lifetime, the best will be the enlightened physiology. It is the physiology that does not bother much about food, eating, the outer world; that which is established in bliss and ecstasy. You see all this, and naturally you say, 'O God! This seems to be a very strong and beautiful physiological structure. Let me choose to work for this.'

Either you may choose the enlightened physiology for yourself, or you may choose to live around that kind of an enlightened being, to be in the same space as that being. But your next decision, the decision of your next birth, will be very strongly towards enlightened physiology. So Ramakrishna's words are true. Even casually seeing an enlightened Master is a blessing. At face value, it may sound egoistic. Only if you look inside logically and understand, you will know that it is a blessing. When I read this before enlightenment, it looked egoistic. When I got enlightened, I clearly understood what it was! Either you are on this side of the game, or on that side of the game. But blessed are those who understand the real inside view of this game, who understand the ideas or truths underlying the game.

Start Now – Clean and Reprogram Yourself!

Annamaya Kosha

You don't even have to wait till death to create an enlightened physiology. If you are seeing me now, you can pick up the Master Card rightaway! You see: every night your sleep is actually death for you. Every day you wake up; it is a new birth for you. If you look a little deeply, every ingoing breath is birth and every outgoing breath is death. Every moment, you are actually dying and taking birth. If you understand this, you don't have to wait till death to create an enlightened physiology. You can start right away!

You can create the enlightened physiology NOW. How to do it?

Two steps to create an enlightened physiology: the difference between *your* physiological structure and the enlightened person's physiology is that he does not carry the *samskaras* from so many births; he has burned everything. So, you also can renounce all the *samskaras* brought from animal body to human body. Basically, the *samskaras* that you bring from the animal bodies are violence and greed – that give rise to sex and fear. Because animals don't have a mind, they don't have intelligence, they have only instinct. But they have *true* instinct. They can save themselves from any survival threat. Also, they can reproduce themselves through physical relationship - sex. They don't do anything else. Your body, the base material for your body, is basically made up of these two engrams – fear and greed. If you can enter into the animal body again, and release these two engrams, your body will be ready, purified, to be programmed for enlightened physiology.

Understand: there are two steps. One is throwing away the engrams you brought from the animal body and other births. The second is, programming your body to have an enlightened physiology - a more positive and energetic physiology. The first part is *cleaning*, and the second part is *programming*. Cleaning, *you* will do. Programming is *my* part. I will do it. I always do my job in the best way, so don't bother! I will do my job. Programming is my job. You just do the cleaning part. Now we will do both the parts.

In the first part, become the same animal that you were. How will you know from which animal you took birth, from which animal you took this jump? In India, they have a technique based on your time of birth. They will predict the animal from which you took birth! It is part of the science of astrology. How many of you have studied your own horoscope? If you have, you will know your animal. There are 27 *nakshatras* or planets. For each planet, there will be an associated animal. Usually, only from the 5-sensed animal, you will take a jump to the 6-sensed human form. So among the 5-sensed animals, they very clearly categorize and classify the animals. But now, how do you tell from which animal you took birth? Just close your eyes, and start visualizing; whichever animal comes spontaneously is the animal.

Yes…I think someone wants to ask a question in the back row?

YOU ARE NOT JUST A BIO-MECHANISM; YOU ARE CONSCIOUSNESS

Q: You said that you disagree with Darwin when he said we came from animals. Now you are asking us to believe that we took birth from an animal.

A: I am not disagreeing with Darwin in the theory that man came from the monkey. I am disagreeing with the part where he says where we will *proceed*. He spoke of only the physical body level. He did not say that there is a part of the human being that has come from the Divine! Understand now: your whole being has not come from the monkey. If that was the case, there is no way of saving yourself. There is some part of you that has come from the Divine. He forgot to touch that part. He forgot to look into that part. He decided straightaway and put the monkey on the throne! From the monkey body, you brought only your engrams, not your consciousness! Your consciousness, you brought from the Divine. This has to be clearly understood. The whole game is about your consciousness. The body is just the vehicle.

According to Darwin, all the systems developed in the West, say that you are just the body. They say you are just a bio-mechanism. No, you are not! You are not just a bio-mechanism. The basic mistake Allopathy did, was to declare that you are a bio-mechanism. If we are just a bio-mechanism, then the person who is dead, and whose body parts are not touched and removed, the medicine put into his body and the medicine put into a living body, should cause the same reaction, is it not? Why is it not so in reality?

There are so many ways in which I can explain why we are not just a bio-mechanism. We are something more than a bio-mechanism. We are not just monkeys. There is an ingredient in us which is taken from the ultimate Divine Energy. You are not just monkeys put together or animals put together. No!

One more thing: today's medication looks at the human body as a combination of several independent parts such as hands, legs, head, etc. If we take the field of dentistry, I am told that there are seven areas in that field! Just imagine: one mouth and seven areas! These seven areas have been further split and have become nine now, I am told. As they specialize deeper, the nine might become eleven. This is the status now, in India. In the West, the specialization is even more.

An American devotee, a dentist, shared with me this information about the high specialization happening in the medical world. If we look at things in such great detail, how can we understand anything holistically? Studying the simple tooth itself may take 32 years! Then, imagine how long it will take to study the rest of the body. A specialist will be able to take care of only that part he has specialized in. Then, who will cure the rest?

Whenever any cure approaches a disease from the outside, the cure can never be total, because the body is not made up of independent parts; it is a whole and holy system. Meditation is what looks at the outside from within. Meditation approaches the body in its totality. There is nothing like meditation separately for the head, hand or stomach. Any meditation technique energises the whole body; the whole body benefits from it. Medical science has grown vastly, with specializations, but medication, along with meditation, is what will restore a positive well-being-ness in the person as such.

We must first understand that the disease is not caused by disorder in any particular organ. Disease is related to the whole body. When only the diseased part is treated, the cause for the disease still remains inside the body; it will not be eliminated. Since medical science looks at curing only affected body parts, the simple approach of eliminating the root cause of the disease is missed.

Annamaya Kosha

Why did this approach of dividing the body into parts come into practice? The reason is that there are many mysteries about the body, which science still does not understand. Many functions of the body remain unexplained.

Whether we understand the body parts or not, it is important to understand these five vital layers in our bodies, which are called *koshas*. It is difficult to understand these five *koshas* as they are of a subtle nature, and based on spirituality. Since we are used to analysing everything through scientific methods, let us try to understand these five *koshas* scientifically.

Let us take the example of an electric cable. What is inside the electric cable? Copper wire. What is inside the copper wire? Electricity. What is electricity made of? Electricity is made of electrons. What are electrons made of? Electrons are made of vibrations and information. What constitutes the information and the vibrations? It is all energy!

Will people not laugh if you say there are five invisible layers inside a cable? Only people who know the science behind it will agree to this.

You can use this example to visualise the five *koshas*.

Now, we are going to work on the physical and outermost layer in which the animal engrams are engraved; we are going to work and cleanse that part. But that does not mean you are only that. You are a mixture of these two. When you clean and release the animal part, the conscious parts start shining or flowering inside you. That is the whole purpose. Now, I hope you understand what I am saying. I think you are clear.

Meditation
- Expel the Animal Engrams

Let us start the work now. You don't even have to know which animal you came from. The animal from which you took birth will automatically come out. Greed and fear are almost the same for all animals. It will be more intense than your human greed and fear, that's all. You can see whenever you are caught in fear and greed that all your civilization suddenly disappears! You feel like an animal! When you are filled with fear or lust, immediately, the animal in you comes out. You become just like an animal. All your civilization, your title, your name, etc, disappear. If you tell someone to video record you when you are expressing your fear or greed, and watch it later, you may even have a fear stroke watching it! Or you may get into an inferiority complex just watching it.

So, instead of unconsciously falling everyday into the animal body, let us fall consciously into it now, and release everything. Let us get rid of it. It is a very powerful process. Take any animal's body, become just that. No one is going to watch you. No video recording is happening here. No photography is happening here. No one will look at you. Everyone's eyes will be closed. Just become that animal and bring yourself to the peak of fear and greed. Just feel the lust and survival fear. React in the way you feel that the animal will react. Let your whole body shiver. Be filled with violence. Be filled with greed. Let your whole body boil with those engrams. Let them all come out. Only then, will programming you be possible for me. Understand that. Unless the strong animal engrams in you leave your system, unless the *pashu* (animal nature) leaves you, you cannot become *Pashupati*! (*Pashupati* is a form of Lord Shiva).

Annamaya Kosha

Understand: you have got so many *samskaras* from the animal layer, because you never allowed them to become reality. These *samskaras* are expressed in your everyday life. You can see it surfacing even when you are eating sometimes. You can see it, when you are angry. When you are really angry, the animal engrams express through you. Sometimes, it may even frighten you. You might wonder, 'What am I doing? What is going on? Why am I so aggressive?' Understand: till you allow the animal inside you to be completely fulfilled and relaxed, you can't escape from it. It should be allowed to come out completely. It should be allowed to actualize itself.

These animal engrams are so powerful. They are called *prarabdha karmas*. This *prarabdha karma* is so powerful. If you allow them to work through you, they will empower you. If you suppress them, they will constantly depress you. You will be fighting with them all the time. Whatever quality you are fighting with, in whatever way you are fighting with yourself, these animal engrams are responsible for it. If you are fighting to control your anger, if you are fighting to stop smoking, if you are fighting to stop drinking, everything is directly connected to this *annamaya kosha*, the animal memories; the *samskaras* which you brought from the animal layer. Even for any addiction, if you are fighting with yourself, the responsibility is this *annamaya kosha's*. Whatever may be the reason for the fight with yourself, the responsibility is the *samskaras* which you bring from the animal body.

Now, we are going to give the opportunity for all those *samskaras* to leave you; all those personalities, the animal layers which you brought with you, to leave you.

The animal in you has to leave you; only then you can become God; only then, the consciousness can shine in you. As long as you are having the physical layer of animal engrams, any small disturbance is enough to awaken that in you; you are there, ready like an animal. See for yourself, how many times in your house, animal-like fights go on when the tempers rise! Look back in your life to see how many times the violent animal nature in you expresses itself. Even though you do not want it, it simply expresses, and later, you regret. Sometimes, during this meditation, people tell me, 'I don't feel like becoming any animal. I don't feel I was any animal. I don't feel anything is coming out.' I tell them, 'Then you must have been a buffalo!' At least become a buffalo and act like one. Use your hand as its tail and drive the flies away! At least become that buffalo.

VEDIC TRADITION – HERE AND NOW

In the ancient traditional *Vedic* system, before the *Gayatri* initiation – the initiation into the prayer for awakening the innate intelligence in the child – he will be made to live in this *mriga shareera* or animal body for six months. In today's modern world, the whole system has disappeared. It has been simply washed away. We can forgive all the injustice done to India in the name of war and plundering; we can forgive even the damage done to our wonderful ancient temples, because they can be rebuilt. But we cannot forgive the destruction of our *Vedic* education system, the *Vedic* tradition that got destroyed during foreign rule. Nearly two hundred thousand *Vedic Gurukul* centers or universities were there in South India alone. Two lakh *Gurukuls* were there in South India alone. Now there are hardly six thousand. In the *Vedic* tradition, when a child takes birth, they will clearly predict, from which animal the child took birth, and what *samskaras* he is carrying. They will help the child release those *samskaras* in his young age itself. Yoga is also one of the ways to release these engrams. That is why each *asana* or posture is related to one particular animal in a certain way. The posture is a technique to release the associated engrams. Then, when the body becomes graceful and pure, they will program it with the *Gayatri* initiation, with the *mantra* and with the energy.

The whole system was lost because the *Gurukul* system was lost. Now, even the so-called *Brahmins,* who wear the *yagmopavita* (sacred white thread), do not know anything of these long-lost traditions. They don't even know why they wear that thread. The science is largely lost. Earlier, by age ten, you are expected to finish all these things. Now, I am giving you a half hour opportunity to live like the *Vedic* times. If you do this meditation intensely, understand, not a single engram will remain in you.

In those times, an enlightened Master would guide the whole process and tell the children individually, which animal engram he took birth from. They would ask him to eat in the same way as that animal; live in the same way; create sounds in the same way. The child would become almost that! There is a beautiful story of a boy *Satyakama japa* in the *Chandogya Upanishad*[1]. His spiritual name is Shwetaketu. I have spoken on this story in the discourse entitled 'The Happening'. He took birth from a cow's engrams. Following the Master's instruction, he went away and lived with cows for a few years, until they multiplied into 1000 cows, and then came back. As soon as he came back, with just a single word from the Master, he became enlightened!

So understand: this is a very powerful process. Of course, unfortunately in today's rat race, we don't have six months to live like animals, but at least this next thirty minutes, we can live intensely to release our animal engrams. Even if you bring out most part of the lust and greed in you, it is enough. The other smaller *samskaras*, I can take care of. From your side, just work towards removing strong and heavy *samskaras* like lust, anger and fear. When you get fear out, your whole body will be shivering. Just visualize how an animal shivers and shiver in the same way. In the tips of your nails and teeth, you will feel violence. Even now, sometimes you can feel this when you look at your in-laws, mother-in-law especially! And this is the case mostly in India. In USA, the relationship between the daughter-in-law and mother-in-law is much better because when they meet, they have time only for work - like babysitting etc. When the mother-in-law babysits, some responsibility is temporarily taken away from the daughter-in-law for those few hours, so she is very happy. Also, they meet only occasionally, so it is not a problem.

Relive and Relieve!

Bring out the whole animal emotion in a live way. Relive and relieve. Re-living is relieving. Choose any one animal. Suddenly you will see two to three animals coming out. Let all of them come out. Just become each animal and live it out completely, that's all. To start with, just feel your head. From your head to your toe, think that you have become the animal. I will guide you step by step. Just one thing, you shouldn't disturb the person next to you.

You might experience a lot of pain and discomfort discarding your identity as a human while doing the meditation. Your

---

1. ancient vedic literature

pain is nothing but the fight between your animal *samskaras* and the higher civilization *samskaras*. When the higher civilization happens to you, when you become civilized, a big layer of conditioning and engrams are kept on you. The fight between the civilization engrams and the animal engrams causes pain and discomfort in your body. If you are just animal, you will not have pain. If you are just human, you will not have pain. When these two start fighting inside you, you start feeling the suffocation.

For example, you will never find a buffalo having knee pain. Fortunately, they are not educated by television. They don't see the advertisements that say: if you have knee pain, call now! They don't see the tablet advertisements that keep calling your attention to an imaginary headache and offer relief from it. If you watch this commercial few times, you will have a headache. You don't have to do anything else. You just need to see the commercial three times, that's all.

Anyhow, the fight between the engrams of civilization and engrams of animals is the pain and suffocation inside your body. If you have asthma problem, just breathe like that particular animal; your asthma will simply disappear! When the engrams of civilization and the engrams of the animal fight with each other, the breathing system starts suffering. Understand one thing: when I make such statements, I am responsible for it. I don't make any indefinite statements. In the last four and half years of the mission, I have worked with almost 1.2 million disciples; at least a hundred thousand patients I have worked with. I don't think any doctor can claim he has worked with hundred thousand patients till now! When I say I worked with these numbers, I mean I have healed them! At least 1.2 million persons have had spiritual initiation or healing. At least a hundred thousand persons have been healed. With that experience, I am telling you, just altering the way of breathing, will heal your asthma. When I make all these statements, I am responsible for them and I mean what I say. Out of the hundred thousand persons, at least ten thousand have been cancer patients.

Let me give you an example for *samskara*. Every morning at 7 o' clock, if you have the habit of having coffee, as soon as it is seven, the bell inside you will ring for coffee even if you are not looking at the clock. The memory, which makes you do the same activity again and again, is called *samskara* or engram. Your walking, talking, standing - everything is based on *samskara*. If you notice, you do all these things in pretty much the same way. There is no variation.

So just visualize the animal first. With the visualization itself so many things will start happening in you. Just become arrogant and violent and express it. Make enough space around you. When you hit another body, just move away, that's all. Moreover, I am going to be here; so I will manage the process.

Start with one animal; you will see that two or three animals come out slowly. Live out all the possible emotions. Just become that particular animal and you will see that all the *samskaras* come out. Every animal has the survival instinct. There is no animal that does not have fear or greed. There is only one animal, or you can say only one *being,* that has no fear and greed, and that is an enlightened being!

Only from an animal you have taken the jump to a human being. In your previous birth, you may have been a human being, but those *samskaras* we are not going to bother about now. We

Annamaya Kosha

want to touch the root from where you took the jump to the human form - and that is the animal form. That is the base material. We are trying to cut that thread so that everything gets dispersed. Just like all pearls are strung on one piece of thread, this base material that is fear and greed, from where you took the jump, is the thread on which all *samskaras* are strung. If you just cut that thread, everything will get dispersed!

Understand one thing: it is the *samskaras* which you brought from the animal life that are haunting you; the animal itself is not haunting you. The same animals might be your pets, but the animalistic engrams are harmful for you. It is a disturbance on the path to enlightenment. In enlightenment, you cannot have any engrams - whether animal or human.

One more thing: you can pick any animal; the instinct of that animal will simply start opening up. That's enough. All we need is the instinct that is lust, greed or fear to open up in you. Literally, the shivering, or the survival threat, or the intense energy flow of lust, should happen in you, just like animals. If that happens, it is enough. The next process, I will take care of.

Understand: express the emotions intensely through action; don't just visualize and leave them.

Whether you are battling with anger, or lust, or greed, any emotion which makes you fight with yourself, anything which you think you are not able to handle, are only from those animals. For example, if you are not able to control your anger, now enter into any animal body. For example, you may feel connected with a lion. Just become a lion and be angry like a lion, literally! Nobody is going to see you; no photography and no videography will be done here. Just become that animal.

Follow Me IN!

You don't know how powerful this process will be; how it will liberate you from so many problems that you are literally dying with. You may be suffering with a particular emotion for the past ten to twelve years. This one session is enough to liberate you from it! I tell you: this one session will simply heal you. I have seen people coming out of not just physical diseases, but years of addiction and mental problems, like lack of self-onfidence, etc. You see: you don't have self-confidence, only because you are not able to win yourself; you are not able to do what you want to do within you. All those difficulties are because you have not completely expelled the animal engrams. Now, all these will simply disappear. They will just melt away when this animal is given the satisfaction, when this animal feels completely total and leaves your system.

Understand: right now, your human existence, the human body, is not completely owned by you. You are not the complete owner of the body which you are having. That is why you are not able to completely control it. There are so many entities who are sitting inside your body without paying rent! Each one is saying, 'This is my portion, get out!' These entities start fighting with each other, and you are unable to do anything about it. You are like a man who is married to four or five women! Sometimes, you talk on behalf of the first wife, sometimes on behalf of the second! Whoever is in front of you at that moment, demanding your attention, you talk on their behalf! That is what is happening.

We are working on the major portion of the *prarabdha karma* which you brought with you when you created this body. That is what working with the *annamaya kosha* means. We are working with the base metal, the base material with which you created the first layer. Then, we will work one by one on the next layers.

So assume any one animal form. You don't have to wonder which is the right animal for you. All you need to do is break from the idea that you are a human being, that's all. Once you break from it, the whole thing will come out. These are all very esoteric and mystical processes, done only when a disciple is really interested and intensely wants to experience the higher consciousness or enlightenment. That is why these methods are not available, in common, for the masses. You may think that you have never read about this in your scriptures. Understand: in religion, you will never learn this. Only in spirituality, you will learn this. These are methods from the esoteric traditions where the science of enlightenment is kept alive, where the living stream is maintained. Fortunately, it is still available and you are fortunate to drink that divine nectar from the very source!

HOW YOU WILL EMERGE

You may wonder: what will I gain out of this process? Once you experience, you will know. I have seen so many people coming out of arthritis; so many disorders related to the body, that they get relief from. They go through this process just once, and they come out of the disease! People come out of so many sexual disorders after one session of this meditation. The problem is really nothing. You have not allowed the animal which is in you to live and leave you, that's all. You have not liberated the animal from your system. You might have taken the human body, but you never liberated the animal! You never allowed those engrams to completely come out of your being, out of your system. So, they sit inside and rule you day and night. When they are inside you, they don't keep quiet. They will simply rule your whole life. They directly or indirectly guide your whole life and all your activities.

Just enter into the process; you will see the relief, or the new space, or the new energy which happens in you. Unless you enter into it, you will not have the confidence to do it. You might have so many questions such as how can I do this kind of meditation, etc. All this is because you have never imagined yourself becoming some animal! Even when kids play animal games, when they imagine they have become an elephant and walk on all fours, you just laugh at them.

Sometimes, people remain frozen during this meditation. They don't want to get out of their frozen identity. They will just sit, and make some humming sound. They must have been buffalos in their previous births! Understand: this is not even a technique. It is a process which needs your 100% commitment.

Even in techniques, I have seen: when I say hum as intensely as possible, people don't hum with intensity at all. So be very clear: if you do that here, we will conclude that you were a buffalo. Actually, I should not say 'you were', you *are*! Then, at least sit in that buffalo body which usually sits silently with legs crossed and chewing something all the time.

Sometimes, you may feel like an animal which you have never heard of, or seen before. Let everything come out. Just live as that, that's all. Move your body, or do any activity just like that animal. Don't just keep quiet. No animal will keep quiet.

Annamaya Kosha

Only human beings will keep quiet. No animal will usually keep quiet. It will be doing something all the time. It will at least be moving its body all the time except during the time it sleeps.

All the emotions which give you the peak experience - like anger, lust, etc, should be lived inside that animal body, because all your peak experiences are driven only by those animal *samskaras*.

Only one thing: don't disturb the person next to you. You shouldn't touch the person next to you. Otherwise, you are free to do anything; you will see that it is an intense catharsis of *samskaras*. Don't think that this is just a psychological catharsis. In techniques for psychological catharsis, they ask you to shout and scream and punch the bag. That catharsis is just for emotions. This is catharsis for the *samskara*s, for the *kosha* itself. We are working with the very base. This will be a thousand times more effective than any psychological catharsis. Psychological catharsis is like cosmetic surgery. But with this, your complete personality will be transformed!

Those who have heart problems, or have had recent surgery, or any major health problem, or women who are pregnant, please refrain from doing this technique. You can come and sit on the side here, and I will guide you all, through separate instructions.

Just express the whole thing. Let the whole body act out and release those engrams from the system. Once it comes out, it will leave your system forever. When it is brought to consciousness, it will leave you. So make enough space for a zoo! And do not be near your husband or wife!

Follow Me IN!

(Meditation starts...and ends)

Om Nithyanandam

Relax. You can open your eyes.

Please remain silent for the next half an hour, so that the silence can work on you. Do not talk. Please be silent. If you use any words, the process will be disturbed. Do not use any words. We will gather here for the next session after one hour. I want all of you to be back here, in one hour's time.

Thank you.

The group gathers again.

QUESTIONS AND ANSWERS

(Questions to do with the animal body meditation have been grouped together for convenience)

Q: During the animal meditation, you said to make sounds like an animal, but I didn't take up an animal like that. I was imagining being a fish.

A: That is not a problem. If your body is alive, that is enough. Fish don't make any audible sound, do they? They might be making sounds, but we don't normally hear them.

Q: Swamiji, I had a vision a couple of times during the meditation. Does it mean that I must have taken that particular animal body in my previous birth?

Annamaya Kosha

A: Yes, surely. If it was a clear vision, a clear picture, then surely it is a *samskara*. It means that those engrams are coming out. You see: your *prarabdha* is like a Pandora's box; when you open each layer, the next will emerge. It is good that you really opened one layer. Good job. If you had at least one violent experience for a few seconds, if you lost the idea that you were a man for even one second, then you have been successful; you have done it!

See, I have an idealistic goal, as well an actual goal, for this workshop. The idealistic goal is: you getting enlightened. The actual goal is like this: I know to what extent you will do the meditations and open up. The technology itself is powerful enough to make you enlightened, but your capability to experience that technology, your capability to put yourself into it, I am aware of...so with that, I have a practical goal also for you. At least, you will have good rejuvenation and release the engrams which you use in your day-to-day life.

The engrams with which you suffer day-to-day are the simple and basic diseases like insomnia, tiredness or chronic fatigue, addictions, etc. Also, you will experience intense joy or excitement. Physical and mental healing is the practical goal. The ideological goal is enlightenment.

This opening that you feel, for even one second, this feeling of being disconnected from your identity that you are a man, itself will release these basic engrams which are constantly bothering your life now. You see, the moment you lose your balance, emotions like anger or lust, will surface. Those engrams will come out first. Those layers will be healed first.

Even *that* will give you so much benefit. That itself will take care of you so much. That is the purpose. So even for a few moments, if you completely forgot that you had a human body, you have done it!

Q: During the animal body meditation this time, I felt like an eagle and many other birds. But I felt strongly about the monkey. It was the only animal that I felt experientially.

A: It means that in one of your previous births, when you took the jump from animal to human form, you must have been a monkey. You might have taken three or four human births prior to this. But just before taking the first human form, the animal from which you took that jump, would have been the monkey!

Q: I got really aggressive during the animal meditation. I just didn't want to let it go until I felt the last drop of it had come out of me. When it happened, I felt like it was finished.

A: Beautiful! You will see from now on, that when you become angry, or when you are possessed by lust, you will not have violence; you will not have the animal nature in you. You will have beautiful grace! When you start expelling all the animal engrams in the path of enlightenment, your body will start acquiring such grace.

Actually in our ashrams, the big problem is that the ashramites don't take me seriously even if I become angry. Even if I shout at them, they will go behind my back and discuss amongst themselves, 'He looks so beautiful even when he shouts!' The problem is, the enlightened body language, because it is devoid of any *samskaras*, is packed with so much grace, that it is difficult

Annamaya Kosha

to show violence in it. Even when we try to show violence, it will not come through as real violence! That is the problem.

Anyhow, you will see that you will not be able to have violence anymore. Even when you become angry, you will not have the monkey violence which was in you all these days. One more thing: even if you get angery, you will be able to quickly recover from it also. See ... when the monkey was sitting inside you, your anger might have taken two days to settle down. But now, when the animal is not there in you, you might become angry, but the next moment it will just disappear! That is the tremendous transformation that this meditation does in you.

Your *annamaya kosha*, your physical body, is not just your body. It is a collection of so many prints together. Now, we are working to make the physical body as your own body, that's all. We are working to bring the whole thing under your control so that you will live completely inside the body. It will be a very pleasant feeling if the body is owned completely by you.

Q: The animals that we have eaten in the past, will they affect our koshas?

A: You see: the suffering recorded in the animal's body when it was killed, *that* suffering will be there in your body if you eat the animal. But the animal's *samskara* itself will not be there. The animal's *quality* will not be there.

Whenever an animal is killed, it experiences tremendous suffering. You see: you are not eating the animal that died naturally. You are eating it after killing it. It is a premature death for the animal. Because it is killed prematurely, it harbors a lack of fulfillment in its flesh. When you swallow that flesh, those feelings will naturally be recorded in you. But the quality of that animal will not get recorded in you.

I have seen that vegetarian people are less prone to depression. Understand: No vegetarian food company is sponsoring me to say these things. I am not sponsored by any vegetarian food producers or companies. From my own experience, I am telling you. I have done enough research in human consciousness. I have worked with millions of disciples. So, I can tell you for sure that vegetarian food helps you, even if you are not a spiritual seeker. Even if you are not a person who is interested in spirituality, even to live a normal life, vegetarian food helps a lot.

Q: Speaking of food, how about plants? We kill and eat plants, too.

A: I have consciously scanned and seen the case with plants. Plants do not have so much of consciousness as to suffer, to experience pain. But animals experience a lot of pain; that's the thing.

Q: What about eggs?

A: In eggs also, there is a possibility of life if allowed to continue. With milk, there is no possibility. People ask me, 'Swamiji, like milk comes from the cow, egg comes from the hen; then why is it that milk is vegetarian and egg is not vegetarian? If you sit on milk and incubate it, you won't get a calf! But if you sit on an egg, you will get a chicken. That is the reason. Somebody may ask if it is alright to eat poultry eggs. Poultry eggs may not have the male part, but the feminine part of life is there. The moment the possibility for life is there, it becomes non-vegetarian food.

Q: Swamiji, I just wanted to know...when we were doing that exercise, it was so powerful...what is your part in the exercise?

A: My part... to open you up! You see: there are many strong and hard nuts in every meditation program. To crack them is my first job. Second thing: those *karmas* which are released, have to disappear. That job too, I do. Moreover, the vacuum spaces which you create within you by releasing the animal engrams will be filled by my presence! Understand: it is a very esoteric process.

Usually when I explain these esoteric processes, it seems like I am claiming too many things. So I generally don't answer these in a detailed fashion. Even this morning, when I claimed that I am enlightened, I saw that a few people were hurt.

But what can be done? Krishna says very clearly in the *Bhagavad Gita*, 'Unless I tell about myself, you can't know. You will not know.' In the same way, whatever you know about me is not enough. If you attend two or three programs, your understanding about me will start developing and expanding.

Just try to attend two or three programs; then you will understand. Your understanding about me will also expand.

See, before the meditation, you had the animal parts inside you. After the meditation, most of those engrams have been released. Now, the possibility of having an enlightened body will be recorded inside you. So, during the moments that you decide your next body, there is a possibility that you will design it to be an enlightened Master! You will ask for the best model. You will rewind and view all the models that you saw. You will see that the enlightened model is the best model, and you will say, 'Okay, let's go ahead!'

Q: Swamiji, I tried very hard to get into the animal meditation but I couldn't, and I don't know if I am doing something wrong by not getting into it.

A: No, you are not doing anything wrong. If you are unable to open up, it means that you are not able to get rid of the strong human identity that you are holding now. Alright, at least in the next few meditations, decide that you are going to break. Even if it is like acting, in the initial level, it is alright. For a few minutes, it will seem like acting; then you will see, that suddenly things open up.

Again, I am seeing families sitting together. Please sit away from each other, for at least these few days. *(Pointing to a particular person)* I think you did a program in Canada, am I right? Yes! I can even tell you where you sat during the program. You were sitting and leaning on the wall; am I right?

You are shocked! You see ... because I don't have any emotional memories, I have access to everything that happened in the past! Emotional memories are like high resolution pictures; they will take away too much of your hard disk space. If you don't have emotional memories, which are actually like high resolution pictures, you can store millions of Word documents in your memory!

In my case, everything is only a Word document, because there is no emotional attachment to any memory. So, I can store, recall, process and handle millions of documents. When I tell some of the *ashramites* to pick up particular books from the library, I will tell them the exact location where to find it! I will tell them: go to the second cupboard and look in the seventh row. Pick up the tenth book, go to the forty second page, pick up the verse in that page and bring it! That is the way the instruction will be given! This is because I have no emotional attachment to any memory. There is no emotional attachment to any one form or any one thing.

Another big problem with me (enlightened beings) is, the moment I am away from a particular country or ashram, I won't even remember the names of the close disciples in that country or ashram. This is a big problem for the disciples! They will start saying, 'Swamiji never remembers us, he never asks about us.' It is not that! I just access different portions of the memory, as and when required, that's all. If you are in front of me again, I will attend to everything concerning you, from where we left off, perfectly!

There is no emotional attachment for me with anything or anyone. But I have so much space, that I make everyone feel special. But everyone wants to be *specially* special, there starts the problem!

This problem is not just with women. It is everybody's problem. At least women are simple, and innocent enough to tell me that they need my attention. These men are very cunning; they don't have the courage to tell, but when they get attention, they will be so happy and beaming!

Q: What form will an enlightened person choose when leaving the last human form?

A: Actually, enlightened people need not take up any form. They have nothing to achieve by taking up any form because they can always operate without assuming any form. When there is something to be achieved with the help of a body and mind, you choose a body and take birth. Enlightenment is like an overflowing fulfillment. When you become enlightened, you feel your enlightenment not just within your own skin, but you feel it alive in every other creature's skin, in every tree and rock. I tell you ... I feel alive inside every skin! How much I feel alive inside this skin, with the same depth and same energy, I feel alive in every other skin. That is the reason why enlightened beings do not need a separate body or form to operate. Of course, when they take up a form, the form is used as a center from which the operations can be performed. Other than that, there is nothing to be enjoyed through this form for them.

Q: Many people say that when they come near you, they know for sure that you are reading their mind.

A: Actually, I never read your mind. I respect your privacy. I never read your mind. Only when people ask for some guidance, I try to help them. But when you come near me, understand that I am alive inside your skin also. The person who is alive inside this skin is alive in your skin also. That is why you feel a little shaken with the feeling that I might be reading your mind.

Q: Human beings who do not see an enlightened person in this birth, cannot chose an enlightened form after death, so what are his options? Another human form?

A: You can become a little more intelligent human being, or an artist, or something like that. Whatever option you saw in your life, from that you will choose the best option.

Q: How many life forms do we take, and what happens after the maximum number?

A: There is no maximum number. Till you achieve enlightenment, you continue to take life forms.

Q: How can I continue to have dreamless sleep?

A: If you do the *Shakti Dharana* meditation before going to bed, it will lead to dreamless sleep. Of course, if you want to have permanently dreamless sleep, even without doing *Shakti Dharana*, you have to get enlightened. After enlightenment, you won't have dreams, because daydreaming stops, and because of that, you will not have night dreams either.

Follow Me IN!

Q: It is very painful for me to carry these engrams. Why are we carrying these painful engrams? Is it because of our ego, or is it an unavoidable principle of rebirth?

A: It is an unavoidable principle of rebirth. It is not just your ego. Your ego can accumulate the social conditioning of this civilization. But the animal engrams that you bring, are a natural thing. Not working to clear those engrams, can be the play of your ego.

Q: What is the practical technique to work on animal engrams? If I feel anger or irritation, how do I come back quickly to my natural self? Do you ever mildly even feel anger, or any of these engrams?

A: This is a beautiful question. If you expand your inner space, you won't have this problem. Even if you have anger, the anger won't disturb you. Your inner space is filled with too many things. Actually, you don't know how to dispose of these things. That's where the problem starts. Disposing can be done only by meditation. Meditation is like cleaning and rebooting your computer!

Q: Do you have anger? When we have anger, we may think of you, but whom will you think of if you have anger?

A: I don't think of anyone or anything, because I don't have a mind. Understand: I don't have inner chatter like you have. What I say to you is what you may call my chatter. It is the only chatter, and it happens spontaneously as I am talking to you. It doesn't take any time to even form inside me. It just comes out, that's all. In the gap that I give between my words, there is no inner chatter going on, like for you. It is difficult for you to understand unless you experience it yourself. Alright, have some experience of this, only then you can relate with what I am saying! For now, understand that I don't have any inner chatter. That is enough. Also, any anger that I show, is only a thread that I bring in to deal with an issue or a person. As such, the anger that I show is not the same as the anger that you display.

Q: *For someone to see the future, does it mean that the future is fixed? Is it already written or decided?*

A: No. It is not already decided, but the course of the future is decided based on your attachment to the past. What happens is, because you are not so intelligent to create a new future, you will reproduce only your past, altered in some way, as the future.

Understand: by constantly jumping from past to future, you will corrupt and pollute your future also, just like your past. You will reproduce the same past in the future; maybe with a little alteration, nothing more. If you scratched with one hand, you might scratch with two hands...a little alteration... nothing much. You will reproduce your same nonsensical past into the future. If you don't take the conscious decision of penetrating the present, if you don't bring down your TPS and settle with the present, you will only reproduce the past in the future. But if you consciously take these steps, you will become intelligent enough to let the future open, and be free for you to create it.

The more your TPS, the more unconsciously you will reproduce the same past into the future. It is like this: when you decide to accept a 2 million dollar home, you accept that the next ten years you will reproduce the past into the future. When you accept the mortgage, what do you actually mean? You consciously decide to reproduce the same past into the future, am I right? In the same way, you will reproduce your past into the future in living also.

Unconsciously, you make so many decisions because of your high TPS, and so you feel that your future is almost bound. If you consciously decide and bring down your TPS to the present moment, your future will be open and available to you for your creativity, for you to design.

One more important thing: when you go through these steps one by one, you will understand how many decisions you made, just because of an unconsciously high TPS going on inside you. Not only that, you will see that you also complained that your future is not under your control! Actually, it *is* under your control. If you come down to the present moment, you can simply break the time shaft. You can simply break the cycle of your future becoming past. That is what I mean by living in eternity, living in eternal bliss. Not allowing this cycle of your future becoming your past, is what I call 'eternal bliss'. You will wonder: how can it be done Swamiji? I tell you: when you don't allow something called past or future in your inner space, when you are just settled in the present moment, the past will not create its footprint in your future, that's all!

As of now, your future has become completely dirty because of your past. Because you are constantly jumping from past to

Annamaya Kosha

future and back to past, the future is continuously getting corrupted. It is like this: in one bowl, there is cow dung, the other bowl has food. If a fly keeps flying from one bowl to the other, from the cow dung to the food and back to the cow dung, what will happen to the food? Little by little, it will start getting the flavor of the cow dung, that's all. The very same thing you are doing to your future also. Your future is like good food waiting to be consumed. Your past, because of your past mental conditioning, is like cow dung. What do you do? You keep jumping between the two, carrying the cow dung to the fresh food.

The reason why you constantly jump is, your past is familiar to you. You feel secure when you think of the past, even if it has not been joyful. It is a familiar pattern to you. You wish your future to also be clear and familiar, without any unknown areas, and so you keep referring to your past and bringing it to your future, with a little change... here and there... that's all. The fear of the unknown in the future, drives you to reproduce the past in the future. But just think: how much can you alter and create your future if your past is the base material out of which you are going to create your future? You might do a little tailoring here and there, that's all, nothing much. You will reproduce the same cow dung, that's all. Actually, cow dung is a decent word that I am using. In fact cow dung is sacred in India. I should be using some other word!

Anyhow, just completely understand the time shaft. So many questions can be answered if you can understand the *kaal chakra*. The time shaft is called the *kaal chakra*. If you see Nataraja, the Dancing Form of Shiva, you will see a big circle behind Him. This is the *kaal chakra*. You will see two big animals symbolically swallowing the past and the future. In the center, He will be dancing. It implies that He is dancing the grand cosmic dance in the 'present moment' between the past and the future.

Q: Can a human be born as an animal in the next birth?

A: Yes, you can consciously decide to be born as an animal.

Q: Why do Hindu gods have animals as their vahanas (vehicles)?

A: It is more than just a mystical representation. In those days, human beings used only animals as their vehicles. There are many philosophical explanations that can be given here. I am giving you a simple one. In those days, human beings used animals as vehicles, and so they designed or visualized gods also in the same way. Also, these *vahanas* represent the individual soul and the gods represent the cosmic soul. So, it is a symbolic representation of the *jiva* - individual soul - being at the feet of the *paramatma* - the cosmic soul.

Q: Why does the spiritual name that you give us, require a legal name change? I take my spiritual search as personal and private, not public and legal.

A: Oh that's nice. Spiritual seeking can be something personal. In that case, there is no need to take a name. It is not necessary. And I don't say that taking a name is compulsory. It is optional. The problem is, unless it is made legal, people don't take it

Annamaya Kosha

sincerely and go by it. They take it lightly. It is a name given by an enlightened Master; it cannot be taken for granted. It represents your very path to enlightenment, if you take it sincerely.

Q: What is it that causes cancer? What can a person affected by it do?

A: Out of the many causes for cancer, the first is, your not feeling completely comfortable inside your body. That is the first thing, the first reason. There are so many other reasons. For example, if your inner space is crowded with too much furniture, and you don't have place for your self, for you to be with yourself, it could lead to cancer. Or, if you are constantly haunted by your past, then your whole inner space is constantly irritated. This could also be a reason. I have spoken on cancer in detailed ways in earlier discourses. Maybe you can try to listen to those discourses. Even in day before yesterday's discourse, I spoke on cancer. Meditation can help you a lot, along with your medication, if you are afflicted with cancer.

Q: There is a nice question here. It says: it is said that lust is like fire. The more you try to feed it, the more it gets inflamed, like trying to put off fire by pouring ghee in it. Does the same hold true for tamas? If you feed it to the maximum, it gets exhausted or does its appetite get stronger? Please explain.

A: Understand; if you feed lust unconsciously, rather if the lust gets fed by itself; only then it grows and grows and grows. It gets inflamed. But ... when *you* feed lust, it will never get inflamed. You feeding the lust means; you know when to say 'No,' and you are saying 'Yes'. Then, it will never get inflamed. The same holds good for *tamas*. When you are saying yes to sleep, say for one month, it will never get inflamed, it will never grow. But ... if *tamas* takes revenge on you, it is depression. You did not allow *tamas* to have its role in your life. Then it puts you in depression and takes revenge on your body and mind. And lust, taking revenge on you, is restlessness. You did not give enough place for it; it just gives you so much of other greed. You see, all greed which you experience in your life, is revenge by lust. When you don't give enough place for lust, it gives you all sorts of greed, like eating, or having more and more new items; more cars, a big house, and so many other items that drive you crazy.

If you consciously don't give enough place for *tamas*, it will completely depress you, and swallow your whole body and mind. *You* consciously giving place to lust or *tamas*, will never inflame them, will never increase them. But when you don't, you are not ready to give place for them, they will take revenge on you, that's all. *It is all about you allowing.*

That is why I tell people to, once in a while, retire from life. We should have a system; where once in three years, a person should be able to take off for one year. That should be the life, say maximum for three years only and not more than that. Then, one year off. No routine, no identity, just go somewhere and do whatever you feel like or don't do whatever you feel like, something like this. See, after all, you can waste one third of your life ... nothing wrong. It's not something so serious. After all, you have so many lives!

Annamaya Kosha

See, all the western religions are teaching that there is only one life. That is why the West is suffering so much. So much of suffering in the West is because these guys are teaching that there is only one life. And it is not true, also. That's the problem. I think you guys can understand. There is so much of time; eternity is there. Don't bother ... just enjoy. Just enjoy! Do this once in a while if you feel like it. Otherwise, there won't be any fun, will there?

I tell only one thing: just do not abuse your body, or waste it by using it for drugs and those things. Otherwise there is nothing like, you should do this, you should do that, you have to finish all these things in this life; there is nothing like that. Just live happily, enjoy, and I can give even some methods to keep your property properly, and secure for you to come back and enjoy. If you consciously build, meaning, if you feel connected consciously, clearly make a map, and meditate on it, and put it in your mind with a clear suggestion. When you come back, all those property owners will be just waiting to hand it over to you.

That's what happened in our ashram. You guys will be shocked if you all know that we have 18 ashrams all created in four years. You will be shocked as to how it could happen! When I came back to Bangalore; the land-owner had the vision that a young Swami named Nithyananda would come, and that he had to hand over this land. He was searching. He came and handed it over. Now, I don't know how many crores (millions) the property is worth. He just came and handed over.

All you need to do is consciously make a *sankalpa*, 'This is my property, I am leaving now, I'll come back and enjoy'. You see, you may all think, 'Oh! I am telling some stories. But this is what happened in my life. Simply I came back and these guys were waiting like trustees. The moment I came back, they handed over the land and went away. And don't even for a moment think that, only in an enlightened Master's case, these things will happen, and in your case it won't happen. No ... not at all. To keep the property, you don't need enlightenment. No, I am really telling you, for all that, you don't need enlightenment. Just a little bit of your mind and clarity is more than enough. A clear *sankalpa* is more than enough. For that, you don't need enlightenment. Enlightenment is far more worthy.

So, just create a strong *sankalpa*, 'These are all mine. I'm leaving now and going, and when I come back, it has to be handed over to me'. And you might think, 'What is this Master, it all looks very funny'. It may look funny, but this is what we call attracting the abundance, the *shree* or the *lakshmi*. Shree means the energy which flows towards bliss. In Sanskrit, shree is the energy which flows towards bliss or the truth, or consciousness. So actually, you can create some property and tell, 'Now, I'm leaving all these things and going. But, I'll come back and enjoy'. You will see that when you come back, people will hand over the property to you properly and sincerely and go away.

The people who are possessing it will be like trustees! And you should also respect them, because they are taking care of it in your absence. All this may look too mystical. But, when you see in life, you will see all these things happening. That's the way it happened at a couple of places; 'We will have land in Chennai near the airport only'. We were about to land; the aircraft was landing in Chennai, and I got up and said, 'We are going to have an ashram. Just now I saw. The land is here. We will have an ashram'. Within a few months, one devotee came and offered this land which was just near the airport. Maybe, when I said, we were flying exactly over that property. I saw below that the ashram is there, and that we are going to have to get ready.

I told one of our *brahmacharis*, 'You should be the spiritual head, so start your training'. See ... don't think it is some magic, or a miracle. It is simple intelligence, which is not very difficult. You see, when you are honest with your thoughts or honest with your *sankalpa*, you will have a clear memory of your past life and everything else.

When I say honest: don't bow down unless you feel the respect. Don't smile unless you feel the love. Take all these things as honest things. Don't smile at somebody having some calculation in the mind. Only if you feel that you have some love for that person, maybe for some reason ... any reason it could be. Sometimes, when you see a beautiful or handsome person, you feel like having a little love. If you have some reason, any reason to smile; smile. If you have some love, smile. If you feel you don't have love, don't smile for mere social reasons. That'll be ugly. A plastered smile is always ugly.

The same way with anger also. When you have anger ... show. Don't show it keeping in mind, that this guy can be exploited easily, or, 'Oh! This guy can't do anything. Let me shout'. I have seen these guys here. If small accidents happen on the roadside, if some old person is sitting in that car, these guys, these young fellows come out and shout. And if they see a big guy, they just keep quiet!

Follow Me IN!

A small story:

One guy came out of a restaurant. He saw his car, which he had parked outside and went inside angered, because so much of paint was poured on it. He came inside the restaurant and shouted, 'Who is the fellow who poured paint on my car?'

One big, strong guy got up, and said, 'Yes, I did it. What do you want now?'

'No, no, the first coat is over. You can come and do the second coat. The first coat has dried. I just want to inform you now, that you can do the second coat.'

See ... that is what we do with our anger also. When we see, we see the person, and play accordingly with our anger. Just be honest with your ideas.

See, one more thing, the *Yoga Sutras* clearly say, if you are honest with your thought flow, you will have a very clear memory of your past life and everything. The reason you are not able to remember your past is because of this simple reason. You see in your own life; if you are very clear in your thought trend, you'll be able to remember the incidents that happened when you were five or six years of age. If your thought trend is too confused, you will not be able to remember even what you ate yesterday. That's the truth. Just keeping the thought trend clear, means honesty. Do only what you feel, and nothing else. Then, so much can be done.

The problem is; in society, you do only when you are paid. Just with this one idea of currency, these politicians have destroyed humanity. By just this one concept of currency, much destruction has happened. Otherwise, we have plenty; we have enough.

The other day, I was reading a nice article. Actually, in one of the states of the USA, Texas, you could accommodate the whole population. There was a nice article which said that the whole world can be kept free; the whole world can come, and we can accommodate the whole population in Texas, in just this one state. I was reading further that if you built homes and developed one state perfectly, completely, you could accommodate the whole world. So much is there. If one country's one state can accommodate, then there is enough land. You can use it for many purposes.

So much can be done in fact. One of the main problems we face is these politicians' ego. And just by this currency concept, the whole thing has gone. Another reason is the concept of 'legal inheritance'; legally inheriting the property. That's another concept which was responsible for this situation. Otherwise, see … we hardly have six billion people. We can easily feed, give clothes, medical care, and literally provide everything. But we are so influenced, and we have so many ideas in our head; nonsensically spending all our money in army... What to do?

I feel that if all these things are taught to youngsters and if they work on themselves and throw all the violence out, they will not disturb other countries. Anyhow, that's why India never invaded any other country. They went out only once to one country, Indonesia. Even that was invaded, they created a city, and lived with the people who lived on that island. They never killed anybody, never invaded any country; never went out to conquer any country. They went only to one country, Indonesia, and to another country, that is, Cambodia. To Cambodia they went, and built a huge temple, which occupies ninety square miles; the world's biggest spiritual structure, the world's biggest religious structure. Even when they went, they did not kill people; they did not fight. They went and built temples.

I was wondering whether these people didn't have enough place in India, to go all the way there to stay. And not just that, the funny part is, the island did not have a single stone. The whole thing was carved in India, shipped and assembled. Even when they went to some place, they only built temples and contributed, because they had nothing else to do. They knew only that one thing, so that's what they did, that's all. A huge Shiva temple was built. I was shocked when I saw it. See, with that one temple, Angkor Vat temple is bigger than all Indian temples. God, I was always proud that my native place has the biggest temple. But when I saw this Angkor Vat, my temple was like one of these American homes, small.

These homes are very small when we compare to some of the houses in India. If you go to the South Indian villages, especially the Chettinad area, each home will be upto 2 lakh square feet. I know a home which has got 1000 windows; it is called 'the 1000 window house'.

People feel very happy if I sit and tell some stories, and tell me, that we can continue doing just this. And that is why these guys put so many questions, also. They start feeling, 'Let him talk and tell some stories; we shall just sit and listen. Nothing else is required. Why unnecessarily doing meditation and all'. Actually if you sit and listen to the stories and jokes, you'll enjoy me *now*. But if you do the meditation also, you'll enjoy me *forever*! You'll enjoy the presence, or this feeling forever.

Chapter 3
PRANAMAYA KOSHA
- Your Breath Layer

Alright now, let us start the next session for the *pranamaya kosha*, the breath layer, which is the next layer. We will then enter into the remaining questions. On a physiological level, the layer of *prana* refers to your circulatory and respiratory systems, the streams of life flowing in you. *Prana* refers to the life-giving energy that you inhale through air, every time you breathe. You don't actually need air to be alive; you need only *prana*.

Prana and the Five Vital Processes

In the morning, I was mentioning that the *pranamaya kosha* does not mean just inhaling or exhaling.

Five processes of *prana* happen inside you:

1. Inhalation

2. The air or *prana* that has gone inside stays in you. It is called *kumbhaka*.

3. The *prana* spreads all over the body. The *prana shakti* – life giving energy - is separated from the air and the energy spreads all over the body.

Pranamaya Kosha

4. The *prana* leaves.

5. The cleaning process happens.

So, the five *prana* processes that happen in you are: inhaling, staying, spreading, exhaling, and cleaning. *Prana, vyana, udana, samana, apana* - these are the five actions of *prana*. Going in, staying, spreading all over, leaving the system, and cleaning. All these five processes put together is called the *pranic* layer. One important thing you need to understand here: the air which goes inside through your nose is not *prana*. Understand the difference between the words *prana* and air. Air is the vehicle. It is just the medium to transport. *Prana* is the energy which is carried by this vehicle. For example, you see many times, a vehicle comes here, unloads something and goes out, is it not? In the same way, air goes inside, unloads the *prana shakti* and comes out. The problem is, because of your restless, unconscious and shallow way of breathing, separation of *prana shakti* from air, that is the unloading time, is not much. Your mind and your *pranic* cycle and the way in which you breathe, are both very closely connected. Because your breathing is so unconscious, the unloading time is very less. With less unloading time, only half of the *prana* gets unloaded and spreads through the body and the air comes out.

Ramakrishna Paramahamsa saw Vivekananda's breathing and said, 'This boy will not live long.' Ramakrishna said very clearly that he will not see age 40. Vivekananda passed away at 39. His breathing was very shallow. Maybe, he consciously designed it that way. After all, he was an enlightened Master. Of course, if he wished, he could have altered the way of breathing. But, he decided to leave the body early. Anyhow, you have not decided to leave the body, so you can change your breathing consciously! You can make it sharp.

Bring In Awareness

As of now, our breathing is unconscious and that is why the unloading time is very less. If you bring awareness to all five *prana* movements, much more *prana* can be unloaded from the air that goes inside and spreads throughout your system.

Civilization has taught us to completely control the activity of 'cleaning'. That is why you end up with stomach problems. In civilization, the natural cleaning process is not allowed. It is considered bad manners, so you constantly have to control yourself. One important thing: you constantly harbor so much tightness in your *swadhishtana chakra* when you try to control the cleaning process. The *swadhishtana chakra* is the energy center below the navel which is associated with fear and it is not good to keep this area tense.

Being too tense takes you away from the cleaning process. Either you should have full control so that you don't need the cleaning process, or you should be in an unconditioned and relaxed mood. Due to social conditioning, you create so much tension in the navel center. This is nothing to laugh about. It is a serious problem. This conditioning is actually killing you. Especially if the breathing is shallow, then the complete unloading and loading of the *prana* does not happen. If the *kumbhaka*, staying of air, happens for a few seconds more, then the *prana* will be completely unloaded, and whatever needs to be sent out, will be sent out. Also, if whatever is to be sent out stays inside your body longer than required, you will be struggling with it.

Pranamaya Kosha

Bad breath, constant sweating, all these things are just because your breath does not have your awareness. You don't breathe with awareness. All the five steps of the breathing process do not have your awareness. That is why there is so much of suffocation. One more thing: because the routine for the entire day is fixed, you have practically lost the spontaneity. Many times you must have seen: you will come down from your bedroom through the same path, sit in the same chair, have breakfast, walk in the same way, get into the car, and only after reaching the office you will realize that you drove for half an hour on the road! Your entire morning routine goes unnoticed by even you!

Recently, I read an article that a person died in an office in India, and for three days they did not realize that he was dead! They thought he was working sincerely. Only on the third day, they realized he was dead. Your routine is so fixed! So your breathing pattern is also almost fixed. But that is not the way life should be. It should be spontaneous, and so should the breathing pattern. It should be alive and deep, with awareness. Bringing a little awareness to the breathing pattern, bringing a little awareness to the *prana*, will create more of a gap between the inhaling and exhaling. It means that the unloading of the *prana* and the spreading of the air energy, which is no longer necessary, will be done completely.

If there is enough gap between inhaling and exhaling, then the cleaning process, that is *apana*, will also be done by its own nature. You don't need any other process for *apana* to happen. You don't even need to do exercise. Generally, working out until you sweat is considered a big thing. If you create a gap between inhaling and exhaling consciously, you don't even have to do any physical exercise, or make yourself sweat. What can be achieved through a workout can very well be achieved through just this. These are the basic secrets of *pranayama*. That is why *pranayama* is considered to bring good health, energy and healing to the body. How does it do so much of cleaning? It is a very simple technique which you are going to do now. It is just bringing awareness to all the five processes, that's all.

You have become completely unaware, especially of the process in which *prana* is spreading all over your body. Every second, the *pranic* energy is spreading from your head to your toe. That is why you are still alive. But you are not aware of it. Not only that, the impulses in our bodies which travel from the body to the brain, and back from the brain to the body, are the physical manifestations of *prana*. It is *prana* that coordinates the activities of the body and mind, and things such as rationality, emotions and other aspects of our personality.

In the Yoga system, they say that when you add awareness to your *prana* process, you will experience the immortal nectar throughout the body. When you become aware of this *pranic* energy flowing throughout your body, only then do you experience the nectar, the joy, and bliss, and this automatically leads to longevity.

Your breathing should be very deep with deep awareness. I don't mean that you should change your breathing forcibly. Forcibly, you can change only for two to three minutes. But if you change the pattern consciously, through deep awareness, you can change it once and for all. Throughout the day and night, the pattern of breathing will be changed. Now we are not going to change it by force. Changing it by force is called *pranayama*. That will help only for 10 minutes. Changing it consciously, by bringing awareness to it, will completely change the breathing pattern, throughout the day and night.

As the duration for which the *prana* stays inside increases, you will become aware of the nectar. Naturally, having awareness and unloading more *prana shakti*, will increase your longevity. That is why we call it *amrit*, which means nectar. In many *Upanishads*, they say, when the *prana* reaches the *sahasrara chakra*, or the crown center on top of your head, it flows all over the body like *amrit dhara* meaning the flow of nectar. When you bring awareness to the five processes - inhaling, staying, spreading, exhaling and cleaning, all the five processes happen beautifully. The sensitivity towards the experience of these five processes, can add more *prana* and more energy to your system. You will be able to experience the life energy flowing throughout the body.

One difficulty with this meditation is that when we do it after food, we tend to sleep. Now, just imagine if I ask you to close your eyes and sit! What will you do? You will simply go to sleep, so just get up now, and stretch your bodies, and then we can sit in meditation. Please loosen your belts because, for the meditation which you are going to do, nothing should be tightly gripping your body.

MEDITATION
- BREATH AWARENESS

Let us start. First, we will take a few moments and become aware of all these five activities, so that we can work on them. Working on this *pranamaya kosha* is more like a bridge to connect yourself to the *manomaya kosha* – mental layer which is the next layer.

Follow Me IN!

First thing: for the next half hour, do not be civilized. Don't bother about social conditioning. It means, you may have the cleaning process happening here. So, if you feel shy, just sit at a distance from everyone! See, you have been civilized all these years, and what you have lost because of that, you don't know. Now for the next half hour, don't hold on to your civilization. See ... when the *pancha prana*, the five *prana* processes happen with awareness, consciously, your whole body will get cleaned, automatically. Not only your nose, even your fingertips will start breathing. Your whole body will become alive. It will start cleaning itself. I have seen a yogi who can breathe through his eyes. He would tie a thread in front of the eyes and blow it through his eyes. He could clean the eyes just with the *prana*. If you can clean your eyes through the *prana*, they will look sharp and shiny!

First, understand at least how the natural ways of *prana* can be cleaned and healed. Your *pranic* layer can be healed and cleaned. Now you are going to inhale, hold and exhale with deep awareness. You will be doing all the five processes with deep awareness. You don't have to put any pressure or force. Don't change the breathing pattern by force. Let it happen as it is happening. Only bring your awareness to it acutely. I will guide you step by step.

First, be aware only during the inhaling part. Even if you miss other parts, it is alright. But don't miss the inhaling part. Just be aware of what is going on. What is happening? When the process happens, what is happening inside your system? Next, we will shift the awareness to the gap between inhaling and exhaling. If you are unaware of inhaling and exhaling, it is

Pranamaya Kosha

alright. But don't miss the gap. Just see what is happening in the gap completely, to what distance you are able to feel the flow of *prana* inside your body at that time. Next, bring your awareness to the exhaling... After that, bring your awareness to the cleaning process. Observe what is happening inside your stomach; what is happening when the *prana* comes in and goes out. Just watch and feel the whole thing.

In this fashion, bring your awareness to every step. The last meditation technique was very wild and strong. This one is a very mild and subtle technique. You need strong awareness to work with this method. First thing, catch the right place for you. Be completely relaxed. Don't be tense, but you can't sleep either. You can't lie down! If you wish, you may sit on a chair, otherwise, you can sit on the ground.

Please close your eyes and tie the eye bands.

Sit in a very relaxed way. Release all tension. There should be no tension around the navel area. Let your navel region be completely relaxed. Do not change the pattern of the breathing by force or by will. Just bring in awareness, that's all. By being aware, if it changes by itself, it is alright, but don't change it by will or by force.

1. Bring your awareness to the inhalation. Do not lie down. Just sit. Bring your awareness to the inhalation. Don't change the breathing pattern by force or by will. Just be aware of what is happening. By being aware, if the breathing changes by itself, then it is ok. You just be aware. (*A few minutes pass*)

2. Next, be aware of the gap between the inhalation and exhalation. Don't sleep, sit straight. (*A few minutes pass*)

3. Now, bring your awareness to the exhalation. (*A few minutes pass*)

4. Now, slowly, bring your awareness to the space between inhaling and exhaling and feel the spreading of *prana* all over your body. Bring awareness to the part where the spreading of *prana* occurs. *Prana* spreads all over your body and makes you alive. (*A few minutes pass*)

5. Now, bring your awareness to all the four processes: inhaling, staying, spreading all over the body and exhaling. Don't sleep. Sit comfortably and bring your awareness to all the four states.

6. Now bring your awareness to the navel center. (*A few minutes pass*)

7. Bring your awareness to all the five movements: inhaling, staying, spreading, exhaling and cleaning. (*A few minutes pass*)

Om Nithyanandam.

Slowly, very slowly, you can open your eyes...

Just go with this very feeling that you are connected to this entire space. Wherever *prana* exists, you are there. In reality, you *are* connected. That is why air pollution affects you, or pure air gives you the fresh feeling. So, just feel connected to the air, to the *prana*.

Pranamaya Kosha

You can have a small break, and get back within half an hour for the next session. Feel connected to the *prana* throughout the next half an hour. Just remember and carry this one feeling - that you are connected; that your whole being is only *prana*.

Thank you.

QUESTIONS AND ANSWERS

(Questions to do with the pranamaya kosha meditation have been grouped together for convenience.)

There are some questions here. Let us go through them now.

Q: I don't think a whole lot of things happened to me in the pranamaya kosha *meditation process, except that I am still in the meditation state and I don't wish to talk to anyone.*

A: How else do you want it to be? You are expecting great things to happen in just half an hour! You are still in the meditative state and you don't want to talk to anyone. Compared to the state you came in, don't you think this is good progress? Is that not growth?

Q: What is it that is supposed to happen when we go through the pranamaya kosha *meditation?*

A: If you have any idea about what is supposed to happen, then you are in trouble. Whatever *is* happening, just *be* with it. If you have a goal, you are in trouble.

Q: Should we inhale through our mouth or through our nose?

A: Only the nose is created for inhaling and exhaling for breathing.

Q: My breath was so slow and shallow, that I felt that I was not breathing at all. I had trouble focussing.

A: See, I told you clearly that you are not supposed to change the breathing pattern. Your breath has become shallow because you don't need too much of air inside. If the separation or the download of the *pranic* energy happens completely, you don't need too much of air. Just a little air is enough, and you will get enough *prana shakti*, life energy.

Q: You spoke of cleansing, but you were not too specific as to what is being purged. Can you please elaborate on it.

A: Don't bother about all that. That is my job. I am doing it.

Q: During the gap, there is a gentle shower of delicate light. It is very blissful.

A: That is what I am saying. You become aware of the *prana* flowing throughout your body. That is the flow of the gentle and delicate light that you are talking about. That is what is so beautiful.

Q: After a few moments of the meditation, there was a feeling that the light inside the body is the same as the light outside. Is this imagination or the truth?

A: It is neither imagination nor the truth. Just go with the *experience*, that's all. There is no need to dissect it with logic.

Q: Why am I afraid of God?

A: Because you are afraid of yourself! Because you are afraid of yourself, you have to be afraid of everything else.

Q: If we have worked with a few enlightened Masters, and each of them has given a specific technique, are we to use them all? Are there any guidelines for working with enlightened Masters who have different styles?

A: You can go around and learn from many of them. It is a nice thing to do. But I feel that when it comes to working, you should work with only one person, because otherwise, you will end up with a lot of confusion. You see: going around and learning is not wrong. Adding more flowers to yourself, or adding more understanding to you, is beautiful. But when you want to seriously work, it is better to choose one Master and work with him, because after a certain extent, it will be a very intense journey. I don't think you will be able to travel in two boats when you enter that zone.

In the initial level, going around and seeing many Masters, and learning from them is alright. Even after you choose to travel with one Master, going around and learning is alright.

There is no problem. But when it comes to working, I think it is better to do it with one Master. See: what we are doing now is an alchemy process. What I am doing to you now is just tiring you; just making your logic tired. That is why, from morning till now, I am just making you sit and sit. Actually, I can entertain you in a much better way! In the first level programs like the ASP or NSP, there is a lot of entertainment. But for this program, I have decided, I will attract only seekers who are really sincere about the process, who don't just come for entertainment.

Q: How do I get rid of fear?

A: Why do you want to get rid of fear? As long as you are alive, you *will* have fear. Fear is a part of life. You feel insecure; you feel the fear of losing something because you have it! So, the very quality of life is fear. So, you should be thankful that you have something to lose. The fear shows that you have something to lose! Otherwise, why will you be afraid? The very fear shows that you have something that you can lose, which can be lost. So you should be grateful that you have something to lose!

Fear can't be lost. You see: fearlessness does not mean absence of fear. *Fear, and the courage to live with it, is what I call fearlessness.* Absence of fear will happen only in the graveyard. Fear cannot be completely absent in you.

Q: How do I live connected to you in everything that I do?

Pranamaya Kosha

A: Constantly living in the *Ananda Gandha* - that is living in an un-clutched way, is the first step. If you are not able to be un-clutched, then listen to the words of the Master through audio or video; or read his books. If you are not even able to do that, then listen to the Master's music – his name. These are the three steps that I can give you for this. So, stay in the pure *sat* – that is with the Self, un-clutched, with pure awareness. If you can't, then listen to the words where the Master is constantly telling you to be un-clutched. If this is also not possible, then by listening to his music, at least remind yourself of the responsibility to be un-clutched. These three methods can help you to be connected to the Master always.

Q: *Since you are neutral in your motivation and goals, what makes you help people? Once we connect to you, and make a commitment, is it that all the experiences that we go through can be interpreted as coming from you. Will peace of mind and heart be felt all the time we go through the experiences?*

A: First thing: this statement: *Once we connect to you, and make a commitment, is it that all the experiences that we go through can be interpreted as coming from you...*

No! When you connect to me, you are connecting to the emptiness. So, you take on the responsibility of all the experiences and happenings in *your* life. Your connecting to me is like *you* connecting to the *higher Self* – your own higher Self. So, you don't have to use such big words like commitment etc. *Will peace of mind and heart be felt all the time when we go through the experiences?* Yes. When you go through the experience, there will be peace and harmony. But you don't have to think that committing to me is like marriage. It is more like a commitment to your higher Self.

Q: Can we remove our rudraksh mala when taking a bath?

A: Yes, you can! But traditionally, we believe that when water, especially warm water touches the *rudraksh* and then touches your body, it has an ayurvedic effect on your body; it heals. It heals the skin. So, maybe you can wear it while bathing.

Q: Can you explain the different lokas like manushya loka, gandharva loka, etc.?

A: When you are in a blissful mood, you are in heaven – higher *lokas*. When you are in your home, you know where you are...! You are in *manushya loka*.

Q: In Indian art forms, they have always portrayed nine rasas or moods that are: shanta *(peace),* veera *(courage),* krodha *(anger),* adbhuta *(wonder),* karuna *(compassion),* hasya *(joy),* bhaya *(fear),* shringara *(love). Do you feel any of these moods other than peace when you are in the nirvanic state?*

A: Understand: I don't feel even the *shanta*. No mood is felt in the enlightenment state. But, I play with all the nine moods as I wish to! If I want to show somebody some mood, I show that particular mood; but there is no mood in the personality itself, in the being itself.

Q: How many hours of sleep are required for an unenlightened person?

A: According to me, whether you are enlightened or unenlightened, four hours of sleep is enough. Anything more than that is laziness. You may justify your arguments with some doctor's survey or research... I have no problem.

Q: You say that there is energy in everything... even in the stones... even in the dead body. Is Life Force different from the energy that you are talking about? What is the difference between the Supreme Consciousness and the Life Force?

A: *You say that there is energy in everything... even in the stones... even in the dead body...* Stones do have energy, but the level of energy in them is totally different. Dead bodies also have energy. There is no doubt in that. That is why, it can go through some changes. You should all know an important fact: even after you are dead, for three months, your nails will grow.

Is Life Force different from the energy you are talking about? No. It is one and the same. *What is the difference between the Supreme Consciousness and the Life Force?* It is one and the same.

Q: How do we remove our engrams?

A: That is what we are doing now!

Q: Is it alright to give the Nithya Dhyaan meditation CD to someone who has not met you or who has not done any of our meditation programs? How often should one do Nithya Dhyaan?

A: The Nithya Dhyaan meditation should be done everyday. You can give the CD to people who have not met me or who have not done our Life Bliss programs, but it is good to have it taught by a teacher first. In the ashram, we have Nithya Dhyaan classes going on everyday. They can attend it. It is just a three hour session. They can learn and then do it. That is the best way.

Q: What is the definition for a spiritual person?

A: One who lives blissfully and keeps others also blissful...that's all!

Q: If I leave my job and spend all my time in meditation and spiritual activities, will I attain liberation faster?

A: Surely, you will. I recommend that you leave your job and put your whole energy in working towards enlightenment. Somebody asked me, 'If I leave my family and spend all my time for enlightenment, will I be liberated quicker?' I told him, 'Surely! Before you, your family will be liberated!' Anyhow, jokes apart, I sincerely recommend you to leave everything and do

Pranamaya Kosha

meditation. Spend all your energy and time for enlightenment. You will surely achieve it faster.

Q: Is bhakti yoga – the path of devotion better, or is meditation yoga better? Which is it that leads to all the yogas?

A: Don't be bothered about all such words. Just take up any one meditation and do it, that's all. Do something; that is more important.

Q. When we offer naivedyam - food to God - we say the names of all these five pranic energies that are prana, vyana, udana, samana, apana. What is the significance and meaning of this?

A: Yes. You say this while offering food, because from any kind of food, you receive these five *pranic* energies. When we offer food to God, we don't offer physical food. The energy part of it is what we offer, so we say it.

Q. After the death of the body, who or what is it, that is choosing the next life?

A: Your consciousness. There is something in you which cannot die. That chooses.

A small story:

In a high school campus, a teacher was walking down the corridor. All the students were wishing her: good morning. The teacher was replying,

Follow Me IN!

'Same to you'. Her friend who was walking with her asked her, 'Why are you not saying good morning, and instead saying 'same to you?' The teacher replied, 'I was also once a high school student. Only I know what they are thinking when they wish me!'

Q. What is the time duration between a soul leaving a body and taking another body?

A: This is a wonderful question. The time taken is three *kshanas*. Understand: not three seconds but three *kshanas*. In the *Vedic* system, time is not calculated chronologically. It is calculated psychologically. Three *kshanas* is the time gap between one death and the following birth. *Kshana* refers to the gap between one thought and the next thought. For example, if you are living with 1000 TPS (thoughts per second), your one *kshana* will be one microsecond! If you are living with 0 TPS, your one *kshana* could even be hundreds of years. So, if your TPS is less when you are alive, after death, you will have enough time to choose the next birth. You can wait for the right time, the right parents, the right place, the right situation, and take birth slowly. But if throughout your life, you lived with a high TPS, intense restlessness, then within microseconds, you will have to move into the next body! Understand the whole concept.

What is the meaning of restlessness and high TPS? It means that you can't live without your body and mind. That is why you have so many thoughts, so much possessiveness over your body and mind. You are caught so much with the body and mind. That is why you harbor so many thoughts. So naturally, you will experience great suffering without a body after death. You will miss your body and mind a lot. So you choose anything that is available first. You say, 'OK, let me just take a jump. Whatever is available is OK.' That is why you choose the body immediately.

Understand this concept of *kshana*. In the *Vedic* tradition, we don't calculate the time chronologically, it is psychological. For example, if you are sitting with somebody with whom you love, even if you are there for five to six hours, you will not know how the time passed by. Suddenly you will see the watch and say, 'O my God! So much time has passed.' Whereas, when you are sitting with someone whose company you do not enjoy, you will feel that time is not passing at all. Every minute will seem like an hour. This is because, when you are with a person whom you love, your TPS drops, your restlessness reduces. Because of this, your *kshana* increases. So even if you are there for four hours, it will seem like only a few *kshanas* have passed by. Whereas, with the person whom you don't like, you become highly restless, and your TPS increases. Your *kshana* becomes very less and you feel a lot of *kshanas* are passing by, whereas you would have been there only for a few minutes! So, time is psychological, not chronological in the *Vedic* system.

Q. So Swamiji, the time is subject to the individual?

A. Yes. *Your kshana* is not the same as another person's *kshana*. So the time duration between one birth and the next birth is subject to the individual. We sometimes stay without taking the body for even three hundred to four hundred years. And it is possible to even prepare the body properly before taking birth, like Bhakta Prahlad from Hindu mythology. He was taught when he was in his mother's womb itself! But we said that we take the next body in three *kshanas*. Then how come, Bhakta Prahlad remained like that for so long? For nine months he was in his mother's womb, learning from Sage Narada. It means that his *kshana* was so long! That is why even now in *Vedic* tradition, we believe that our one year is one day for the *devatas* (heavenly beings), because they stay at such low TPS! They stay at 20 to 30 TPS. So our one year is one day for them! The aging process does not happen when your TPS is low. This is the best technique to be graceful and beautiful always. The aging process will not be fast if your TPS is low. That is why our one year is one day for the *devatas*.

Even today there is a temple which belongs to the *devatas*. It is in South India. It is called Chidambaram temple. It does not belong to human beings. It belongs to the *devatas*! So, in a year, the *puja* (offering) is done only six times! In all other temples, every day, the *puja* is done six times! But here, in the Chidambaram temple, the *puja* is offered according to the *devatas'* calendar, not according to human beings' calendar, and hence the long gap in the offering. The TPS is different. When the TPS changes, your *kshana* changes. We are trying to replicate the Chidambaram temple in Seattle, USA. The first Golden Temple in the USA will be in Seattle!

Q: Is that why we do puja *for elders who have passed away, once a year?*

A: No. That has nothing to do with this. You offer once a year because of your own laziness. You can't be sure whether the elders had a low TPS or not. *Devatas* are at low TPS. We can be sure of that. It is not sure that the elders had a low TPS, because it depends on the way in which they lived. Understand the basic thread: if you live without possessing your body and mind too much, your TPS will be low. So after leaving the body also, you will not suffer, because you are already trained not to possess your mind and body too much. If you are possessing your body and mind too much, it means that you can't be without them. So, the TPS is more, the need is more, and the urgency to get into another body and mind is also more. This is the essence of the whole of Spirituality.

Anything which reduces your TPS is spiritual practice. Anything which increases your TPS is material life. Sometimes, when two persons are in tune, even a beautiful relationship between them can bring their TPS down. In *Tantra*, two persons who are completely in tune with each other, without any fantasies about each other, accepting the other as they are, are equal to Shiva and Parvati – the Divine couple. They will help each other enter into *samadhi*.

With deep sincerity, even an ordinary relationship can lead to low TPS. Without understanding or sincerity, even the *puja* that you offer to God can lead you to restlessness and a high TPS. I have seen so many people getting restless and finishing the *puja* quickly. They will run out from the *puja* room and not even think about the *puja* room until the next morning! Even the next morning, they will get into the *puja* room just out of fear that if they don't offer *puja*, things might go wrong that day. Even the so-called lowest activity can lead to low TPS if done with sincerity. Anything leading to low TPS is spiritual practice, and anything leading to high TPS is materialistic activity.

Q: In one of the discourses, you said that after the soul enters the body, it takes 13 days for it to gain consciousness.

A: No. I said: 13 days is the time taken to completely ascertain that all parts belong to him, that all parts are his body parts. Do you understand what I am saying? Understand this one example: sometimes in the early morning hours, you will neither be completely sleeping, nor be completely able to take control of your body. You will be awake, but you will feel that you are not able to move your body completely. Suddenly, you will see that you are trying your best to possess your body! It is that same moment that will be extended to 13 days in the context of what I am saying. You are neither out of *shushupti* - deep sleep state - nor are you fully awake - *jagrat*. So, it takes a little time to possess your body. It takes normally 13 days for any being to possess the whole body. During those 13 days, you need to keep that person in a healing and loving space. It will be almost as if somebody is sitting on your chest. You will be just waiting to enter into your body with all your power. In the same way you will be struggling for 13 days. But if the right enlightened being creates a beautiful space for you, the struggle will not be there. It is because of this that we have the 13 day ritual, after death or after birth. The ritual is done because whether the person has left the body, or the person is born, their baggage needs to be handled, and they need an open place and a conducive ambience for it.

Q: Swamiji, is this TPS significant at the time of death, or when you are alive?

Pranamaya Kosha

A: When you are alive, a low TPS will keep you more in the present moment and blissful. The lowest TPS that you have experienced during your entire life will automatically pop up at the time of death. The lowest TPS you experience will be the strongest experience in your entire life. When death approaches, when you start feeling the suffocation that you are no more going to be alive, automatically the lowest TPS experienced in your life will open up. That is why, at least once in your life, you should experience 0 TPS. You can then be sure that you can leave your body with high consciousness. There is a beautiful verse by Krishna which says: whatever you remember at the moment of your death, *that* will decide your next birth.

Q: Swamiji, will I be conscious when I die?

A: If you have experienced 0 TPS at least once in your life, you will be conscious when you die, otherwise, you will not be; you will be only unconscious; you will just fall into coma and leave your body. That is the worst thing that can happen to a human being. Your whole life is a waste if that happens. If you die in coma, it means that the entire time that you have lived has been wasted. That is why I emphasize: do not miss meditation in your life. The half hour, which you spend everyday in the initial level, may appear to be fruitless, but in the end, only *that* will be the useful moments for you. Only those moments will pop up and save you. So don't miss.

Q: Swamiji, does the soul enter the body during conception?

A: No. The normal soul enters just before birth, because as I told you earlier they don't wait for more than three *kshanas.* as I told you earlier. One *kshana* will be usually less than a second. Only highly conscious souls have enough gaps - like Bhakta Prahlad.

Q: So the learning in the womb happens for only highly conscious souls?

A: Yes. It happens only for the highly enlightened souls, not for the ordinary souls. Enlightened beings choose the right parents, the right place and the right date to take birth.

Q: What do you say about coming back from coma?

A: It is like a part of life. There is nothing right or wrong about it. There is neither something positive nor negative about it. Coma is like falling between the fourth and the fifth layers and coming out of it, that's all.

Q: In a television show, a guy named John Edwards talks to the souls of the audience's near and dear ones. He says, they are wandering and trying to connect with us.

A: No. No soul is wandering or trying to connect and talk to you. They have all already taken a body. Some souls who die prematurely in an accident may be in this state. You can contact souls if you wish to. For example, you would have been somebody's father in the past birth. Now, they can contact your unconscious memory and dig out information. But it will create suffering in you. So, never try to contact your near and dear dead ones. It will disturb your flow of life, as well as their flow of

Pranamaya Kosha

life. Suddenly, you will see that you are drained; you feel tired. These kinds of things can happen, when you try to contact your dead near and dear ones. This is like forcibly entering into others' archives. Don't do it.

Q: You said we should try to bring down our TPS. Then what is the purpose of thought?

A: I think you missed the morning session in which I gave a detailed description of TPS. You see, when your TPS is too high, your desires will be too physical. You will only experience the joy from the tip of the five senses - tip of the eye, tip of the nose, tip of the tongue, tip of the ear, tips of the sense organs. Your desires or pleasures will be too gross, and you will be settled in the *annamaya kosha* or physical layer. When your TPS drops a little, your desires will be a little more subtle. You will enjoy fantasies but you may not ask for much of physical pleasure. If the TPS is further lowered, your desires may be a little more subtle, like they might have to do with name and fame, recognition, etc. - the mental layer desires. As the TPS comes down further, again, your desires also get more and more subtle. At the lowest TPS, everything disappears... Pure energy, without desire, is enlightenment. A pure and intense excitement without desire is enlightenment. That happens at zero TPS.

Q: I feel more body aches, especially today.

A: I think it is because you are sitting on the floor. Sit on the chair.

Follow Me IN!

Q: How come we are asking the same questions?

A: Because you are the same. You have not transformed. Humanity is the same. That is why you ask the same questions.

Q: Do animals have five koshas?

A: No. They don't have fully developed *koshas*. They may have the *annamaya kosha* and *pranamaya kosha*. Actually, they don't have even the entire *pranamaya kosha*. All the five *pranic* movements do not happen in all the animals.

Q: Where are the samskaras stored?

A: The *samskaras* are stored in all five layers, not just in the *manomaya kosha*.

Q: Is it possible for a person who has led a life of meditation to go into the state of coma before dying?

A: Leading a life of meditation and prayer are not the right words to use in this context. If he has experienced 0 TPS even once, he will not fall into coma. That is the way to say it. There are thousands of people who claim to be leading a life of meditation and prayer, but who have never achieved a state of zero TPS even once. And there are many people who have not led a life of meditation and prayer but who have achieved zero TPS, at least once!

The 0 TPS experience depends on your courage and decision to experience yourself. It is not even dependent on your regular

Pranamaya Kosha

puja, prayer, or meditation. I have seen these fools: morning to night they will be sitting and ringing bells in front of their gods, or reading some *Sahasranama*. Understand: with a deep feeling of connection or devotion, if you recite the Lord's name even once, it is more than enough. Without that feeling of connection, these people, the moment they start reading the *Sahasranama*, the first thing they do is, check the line number!

Anything that you make as a daily ritual will become an unconscious act. I am not debunking tradition. I am a big supporter of tradition. But your mind is such that it will just take it for granted. I know the basic trend. After five minutes, automatically, you will look at the line number. That is the problem. The moment you do that, the whole thing is wasted. Just the regular meditation or regular prayer does not mean you had the zero TPS experience. Zero TPS experience has something to do with a conscious decision and strength to experience it. It has nothing to do with the outwardly experiences and meditation that you are doing.

I always tell people: even Nithya Dhyaan, the everyday meditation that I prescribe for everyone, could be made a ritual. You can sit and do it without even being aware about what you are doing, and at the end of the meditation, nothing would have happened.

Q: But most prayers require some degree of repetition.

A: No. Prayers don't need any degree of repetition. Prayers are supposed to be giving you the experience of feeling connected with the Divine. That is why I have designed Nithya Dhyaan in such a way that you will not be just sitting all the time. Every six to seven minutes, I will change your position and activity... just to awaken you. Of course not just that... the chaotic breathing and humming in the Nithya Dhyaan meditation, will simply shake the *annamaya* and *pranamaya koshas* to awaken a higher-level consciousness. Earlier, there have been meditations which were constant for 30 minutes, and I have always found people falling asleep.

A small story:

This really happened in my life. In my wandering days before enlightenment, I reached a place called Omkareshwar. It is the place where the great Shankaracharya became enlightened. It is a beautiful place. I was staying there in the monastery. Early morning, all the monks are supposed to sit and meditate from 5:30 to 7:30. At 7:30, the sun will rise, and then there will be a gong from their bell. All the monks will roll up their mats and go for the next activity.

One day, a young brahmachari (aspirant on the path of sannyas) who was sitting in front of the gong, slept and fell on the gong. All the other monks got up, rolled up their mats and went away! Everybody thought that they might have gone to sleep, and hence lost track of time! All the monks were so confident of this, while getting up to leave. Not a single one suspected that something had gone wrong, and that the bell had rung much earlier than the usual time!

The same thing started happening with the *Mahamantra* meditation. That is why I decided, no more silent techniques. The reason why you fall asleep is, unless the catharsis happens, you can't just sit. Everything has to leave you, only then the silence can happen in you. The insanity has to come out, only then the sanity will happen in you.

Pranamaya Kosha

Q: Swamiji, anything given by an enlightened Master is supposed to help others get enlightened. Then why is Sahasranama *not helping?*

A: Understand, the *Sahasranama* was given for Bhishmas, for the people of those days. At that time, people were simple and innocent. They were not so complex. They didn't have all these cerebral layers. They didn't have television, and did not get stressed out working with computers. Your entire constitution is different today. Not only the constitution of the country, the constitution of the whole system is different. That is why Patanjali's techniques cannot directly help now.

Enlightened Masters have visited planet Earth from time to time and updated the techniques as and when needed. That is why there are so many techniques that are not directly useful today. It is not that I have not learned from Patanjali. At the age of three, I started learning from Patanjali's teachings. I had a master by the name of Raghupati Yogi. If you read his biography, you will know: he was a direct disciple of Mahaavtar Babaji. He lived with him. He was in Tibet and he was in Gaurikund where Baba gives *darshan* to people. He lived there, and learned all these things. But straightaway, they are not going to help you now. Your system needs to be prepared, even to go through the Yoga system. Your system is not so pure and innocent. See, Patanjali says: just sit and remember the *Om, Pranava* – the primordial sound - and your mind will enter into *samadhi*. Now you tell me what will happen. If you just sit and remember *pranava*, where will you enter? You know which *samadhi* you will enter! You will be fast asleep in no time! Your mind and your whole setup are totally different. Too many things have been put inside your being, and that is the reason why you are still struggling.

Q: I gather that the subconscious mind is initially created consciously. I also gather that things done with consciousness cannot go wrong. How does the subconscious get programmed or wired incorrectly.

A: There is some part of you, that you don't want to remember again and again. Let me give you this example: Let us say you are sitting near a swimming pool and sipping a cup of coffee. Suddenly, some thought or person whom you don't want to remember or think about will come into the mind. Immediately, you turn your face and attention away from it. Sometimes, you even say verbally, 'Why am I thinking about this guy?' Now, when you don't want to remember a thing or a person, you push it into the subconscious. These things get settled and become like a frozen rock. That is the subconscious.

Q: How do we set goals without letting the past dictate the future?

A: This is a good question. When you bring down your TPS, a new intelligence will suddenly happen in you, which causes you to perform without setting goals. That is what I call Intuitive Management - managing through intuition. It needs patience and practice. That is why people are not able to trust, that something like Intuitive Management is possible. People who live around me can see it happening. I am running an organization with centers across many countries, and we are continuously expanding as well. Just three days ago we started an ashram in Malaysia. So much is happening, but we never plan like the corporate world. Spontaneous decisions are just made. Intuitive Management works continuously. Living around

Pranamaya Kosha

the Master can give you the courage to see that it is possible. For you to run your day-to-day life, to pay your bills, to pursue your profession successfully, and to create wealth, your mind is not needed. It may be a little shocking to hear this, but just try it out. You will see that it works.

Q. When I watch television and lose myself in it, I feel drained of energy.

A: This is a dangerous thing that has happened to humanity. Somebody asked me, 'Swamiji, when did the age of *kali* (the fourth quarter of time, believed to be the degradation era) start?' *Kaliyuga* is supposed to be the Dark Age. I tell them: the day television entered your home, the Dark Age started.

See, let me explain. Your eyes can tolerate only 16 frames per second while watching anything. Understand: if you are driving at 60 miles per hour, maybe 10 to 12 frames per second will change in front of you. If you are driving at 100 miles, then maybe 20 to 30 frames will change every second. Through the television, computer or cinema, you experience at least 35 frames per second. It means, there is twice the regular stress.

When so much of stress is put on your eyes ...

You have a certain intelligence, a certain logic, which analyzes whether what you are seeing is right, or it is just an illusion. There is an intelligence in you that does this. We call it *chakshu*, which is the energy which sees through the eyes. You are not seeing just by the physical eyes, you are seeing *through* the eyes. That *indriya*, that *chakshu* which sees through the eyes, usually calculates whether what it is seeing is real, or it is just an illusion, a hallucination. It enables you to differentiate between the castle in the air, and the real castle. It gives you the clarity of whether it is reality, or an illusion. This *chakshu* is put to sleep when the frames per second is 30 or more. So, whatever happens during that high rate of frames per second, your logic accepts, without analyzing whether it is the truth or not. That is why, any advertisement which is put inside your head through the television, will cause you to unconsciously go to the shop, and ask for the same product that was there in that advertisement!

When the frames per second is high, you will be unable to differentiate between reality and illusion. That is why you can see that even your BP (blood pressure) changes along with the program. Am I right? You cry, you laugh, you do everything along with what you see on the screen. You know very clearly that the actor who is dead in the screen is actually alive otherwise. But when the television is on, you don't remember all this. Your logic does not come into play at all, and you even start shedding tears. It means, beyond your logic, your whole intelligence is put to sleep, and you respond to what you see directly. That is the worst thing that can happen to you. That is the most dangerous thing that can happen to a human being. *Beware of the television*. That is why you are drained of energy, and sometimes fall asleep watching. You are raised to a high TPS. There is so much of restlessness when you are watching the television.

Q: But we also watch your discourse DVDs.

A: Watching my DVD discourses cannot be compared with watching the television. When you are watching me, an enlightened form is getting into your inner space. That makes all the difference. It can never damage your consciousness. In fact, it will nurture your consciousness.

Q: *When I am in your presence, or when I am doing mission work, I feel more energetic.*

A: Yes, because the whole thing is to do with superconscious energy. That is why you feel more energetic.

Q: *Is not my TPS low when I am watching television? Then why am I feeling tired?*

A: No. Your TPS is not low when you are watching television. It shoots up. When you connect with an enlightened Master, your TPS drops.

Q: *I felt that the time taken for the various stages, that is for inhalation, holding, spreading and exhalation, were very short. I consciously had to slow down breathing.*

A: If you felt that the time was short it means that your TPS was low. If you felt that the time was more, it meant that the TPS was high.

Q: *Can the* rudraksh *bead be worn by everybody? From a young age, it was taught that it was very sacred and it is not to be taken lightly.*

A: Even if it is sacred, you can wear it; there is nothing wrong in that. In fact, *because* it is sacred you should wear it! If the *rudraksh* is sacred, you are also sacred. You are also divine. Why do you think that you are not divine? So, divinity can reside on the divine. You are not *shava* (corpse), you are Shiva. So wear the *rudraksh*.

AUXILIARY SIMPLE HUMMING MEDITATION

Alright, should we finish one more meditation? It is a simple technique. It is not even a technique; it is just a process. Let us finish that and then, I will answer the remaining questions. Then, you can go for dinner.

It is a very simple process. Just intone the sound of *hmmm* along with your inhaling and *smmm* along with the exhaling. It is a very simple process. We are just trying to separate your inner chattering and the *pranic* layer. If you intone this *mantra*, you will not have any other word or any other thought during your inhaling or exhaling. When you inhale, slowly make the sound *hmmm* along with it. It is not chanting, it is just intoning. When you exhale, intone the sound *smmmm*. Intoning means: just mentally going with the *mantra*. Do not miss even a single breath. Just intone this *mantra* for the next few minutes. This will separate your *pranamaya kosha* and *manomaya kosha*. When this happens, it will be easy for us to do the process, the programming of the *pranamaya kosha*.

Please sit in a relaxed way. Tie the eye band over your eyes. Just sit. Do not alter the way in which you breathe. Just intone *hmmm* along with your inhalation and *smmm* with your exhalation. Do not chant. Just intone...just internalize.

(The meditation is done while Swamiji sits looking at the question slips. He ends the meditation shortly.)

Pranamaya Kosha

Somebody is asking questions about ghosts! There are so many questions. Alright, it is time to end the session. It is quite late in the night. You can go to sleep now. Tomorrow morning, we will see the rest.

If you go to sleep now in this same mood, you will be tired tomorrow morning. Just stretch your body, be a little fresh, then go and sleep. If you jump a little now, the second layer energy will be awakened! Actually, if you want to get up fresh in the morning, jump for ten minutes before falling asleep. Or, sing or dance; do something very active before going to sleep. Then, lie down and fall asleep. You will get up in the same lively mood! Actually, *how* you fall asleep, with what consciousness you fall asleep, with *that same* consciousness, you will come out of sleep also. After you have finished eating and feeling full in the stomach, don't go and sleep. Just get up and stretch your body a little, and then go to sleep.

Please be here tomorrow morning at 7 o'clock for the *Nithya Dhyaan* meditation. Now, please get up. Stretch your body fully. Up! Up! More! Alright, enough. We will meet tomorrow morning.

'Just Sitting' again...

Before entering into the next session, let us enjoy this beautiful morning. Let us just sit. Let us allow the *Upanishad* to happen. *Upanishad* means, just sitting (at the feet of the Master). When I say just sit, I mean - no *mantra*, no meditation, no technique, no concentration, no awareness method. Just sitting, that's all. Even if you are restless, even if your mind is asking how to just sit, don't bother. Just sit as you are. Let your eyes be closed.

Follow Me IN!

Just sit. Close your eyes.

(Some time passes)

Relax.

You can relax.

Just sitting for no reason, without any technique, can do so much in you. The process can happen so beautifully by just sitting. In Zen, they call it *Zazen*.

The 'just sitting' is a thousand times more effective than any other technique, because in any technique, in any method, you will be busy. I can't catch you *as you are*, but in 'just sitting', I can catch you *as you are*. Even if it is a little difficult, just struggle with that difficulty and sit. Only then, I will know exactly in which space you are. Then, it will be easy for the Master's presence to work. The Master's presence is like an intense energy that will start working on you if you are as you are.

When you are sitting as you are, the process happening will be really deep. I can see from the morning until now, there is an increasing silence happening in each of you! When you just sit, the presence of the Master works so much on you. If you are already working with something, it becomes a little difficult for me to work on you. With you just sitting, I can do a lot more on you.

QUESTIONS AND ANSWERS

There are so many questions this time! I think there are three bunches of papers. If I answer all the questions, I think we will

Pranamaya Kosha

end the session only the day after tomorrow! Anyhow, I will try to answer as many of them as possible.

(Questions related to the humming meditation and TPS have been grouped together for convenience.)

Q: Thank you Swamiji for such a wonderful experience. Ten years ago, I had this similar experience when I was meditating on Lord Shiva.

A: That's nice. In India, we allow people just to be in that state for some time. Not only that, the ambience there is totally different. Also, we have four days time for this same program. You see, you need at least four to five days to sit with the Master. Here, the life culture does not permit that. You have to leave tonight. That is the reason why you can have only a glimpse. No sooner than you have that glimpse, I have to say, 'Come down from the experience and relax.'

Q: I do not have words to explain how I felt in those moments. I wanted to die or vanish at that very moment.

A: That is the beauty of enlightenment or meditation! When you experience even a mild *satori*, you feel like you are fulfilled.

Q: When I started doing the hum sum meditation, tears started pouring from my eyes. I was becoming very emotional. I had to control my mind up to stop the tears.

A: No, you should not have done that. You are not expected to bring in your mind. You are expected to go through the process – whatever it is.

Q: I want to be in that state always.

A: First fear, now greed! Because of fear, you stopped it. Now because of greed, you want more! Anyway, you should not have stopped the experience. But neither should you have greed to be in that experience always. The process should happen, and it should happen in whatever way it happens. Then the experience itself may not stay, but the juice or the essence of the experience will stay inside you.

Q: Is this hum sum mantra same as soham?

A: No. *Hum sum* is the original *mantra* from the *Paramahamsa Upanishad*. *Soham* is the version that was developed later. The original *Upanishad mantra* is *hum sum* only. A person who is established in That, is Paramahamsa. Later on, versions like *soham* were developed.

Q: During meditation, even if there is a mild sound, it startles and shakes my whole body. Is it fear or is it normal?

A: It is fear.

Q: I am experiencing some satvic (goodness) feeling. Actually what I mean is, I am experiencing a passive and sad feeling, and I don't feel like reacting to even anyone who hurts me in any way. Is this a healthy feeling for a person like me who must lead a worldly life and not a sannyas life?

A: There is nothing called a worldly life or a *sannyas* life. If you are comfortable like this, just leave it, that's all. It will pass. Don't hurt people and don't think that the whole world is waiting to hurt you. It is mere foolishness to think that people are waiting to hurt you. It is the enmity in you that you project on others, and attract it towards yourself again. It is a play of the mind.

Q: Is not TPS reduction like having a popup blocker?

A: No. Popup blocker is a forced phenomenon. Here it is not forced, it just settles, that's all.

Q: Is there a correlation between someone's frequency and TPS? Can two people with 100 TPS have different frequencies?

A: No. There is a correlation between the frequency and TPS. If you and your husband are at almost 100 TPS, both of you will have a beautiful life. Both of your desires will be almost the same. See ... when both of you are just enjoying a physical level relationship, your desires will be only physical; you will have just physical fulfillment, that's all. Both of you will meet and relate for maximum half an hour, not more than that. Then the fight will start. Both of you will be bored with each other. Only for that period, you can entertain each other. After that, both of you will take the whole thing for granted. How much can you entertain in the physical layer? Maximum, for half an hour, not more than that.

Let us take the next higher level where both of you have the same taste in art. Let us say, both of you are singers, or both of you are dancers, or both of you are painters...some art, some similar passion. Then the relationship can be a little deeper. You will start relating with the *manomaya kosha* — the mental layer. And there is a possibility that you may entertain each other or feel fulfilled by each other for at least 20 to 30 years.

Next, if both of you are seekers, if both of you are on the seeking path, then life and relationship will be eternal. You will feel that the other is fulfilling or enriching you so deeply. You will feel that the relationship is just fabulous.

Q: At zero TPS, if you can see your future, can you choose to change it?

A: You have the full freedom to change, but you will not be encouraged to change it at that point in time! When you are in that state, you will experience so much freedom and truth, that you won't even bother to change it! Just by your will or presence, it will automatically change - whatever needs to be changed. You won't even bother to forcibly do anything about it. That is the beauty of the truth! Now you feel that you want to change it, but when the truth actually happens to you, you will not be affected by this thought at all, and so you won't bother to change your future.

It is like this: if you know that these rooms are locked, and that you can't go out, then, you will just be dying to go out and get some tea or do something else, is it not? But, if you know for sure that the door is open, then you will just sit here in a relaxed way with no thought of escaping! It happens in the same way.

Q: *Sometimes, when I connect to you, I cry a lot. At that moment I feel that I want only you. Does it mean that I have zero TPS at that moment?*

A: No, not zero, maybe 50 or 40. In zero TPS, you won't even feel that you and I are separate. Only if you feel that you and I are separate, will you think of wanting me. In zero TPS, you and I will not be separate.

Q: *Is there a name in Sanskrit for the divine cosmic energy?*

A: Yes. We have the name *Parashakti*. That is the name.

Q: *Where do I learn about this divine cosmic energy?*

A: You are learning here, right now. What else do you think you are doing here? *(laughs)* Do you think you are learning to cut vegetables?! I am not teaching you how to cut vegetables for this long! You are learning only about the divine cosmic energy.

Q: *I have always been wondering about the purpose of my life.*

A: Just understand: you don't have to wonder about the purpose of life. Just constantly being in the *mood* of wondering *is* the purpose of life! Nothing else. So you are on the right track. You are saying that you have always been wondering about the purpose of life. Instead, just be *wondered* about life, that's enough! Then you automatically achieve the purpose of life. See, if you wonder about the purpose of life, you will never achieve it. Just wonder about life *itself*. Then you will achieve.

Q: **You said to wonder. I can't stop wondering how people can be so cruel and ignorant and why people have to suffer so much in such horrible ways.**

A: It is not wondering that you are doing; it is worrying *(laughs)*. Wondering is different, worrying is different. You are not wondering; you are worrying. You may use the word wondering, but you are actually worrying. Relax from it.

Q: **What is a good question to ask you and what is your answer? (laughs)**

A: Hmmm…I am just thinking what is a good question to ask me… I think silence is the right question. And silence will be the right answer! That is the good question or the best question you can ask, or the best answer that I can give you.

Q: **When I feel your bliss, I become immediately, intensely aware of it and almost immediately, the experience stops. How do I stop the thought so that the experience can continue?**

A: Don't be greedy to be in the blissful state always. Then it will stay forever. Only your greed stops it.

Pranamaya Kosha

Q: Is it true that once enlightenment is achieved, one will no longer dream while sleeping?

A: Yes. I have had no dreams after my enlightenment; no daydreams or night dreams.

Q: What is the purpose of siddhis (mystical feats)? Do you agree / disagree with Masters who perform them?

A: It is up to them. There is no need to pass judgment on that. Sometimes, when it is absolutely necessary, such feats express through enlightened persons also. In my case, if it expresses itself naturally, then I allow it. But otherwise, I never express anything like that. Many times, people come and tell me, 'Swamiji, from your photograph, *vibhuti* (holy ash) and *kumkum* (vermillion) is constantly coming.' I tell them that it is good.

I neither directly agree with all this, nor disagree. I don't directly agree because if I agree, some people loose the idea of enlightenment and get caught with these types of things. I don't disagree also, because sometimes for some people, these types of things will be a source of big inspiration on the spiritual path. It makes them feel connected to the path. Sometimes, when a person sees even one small miracle being performed in front of his eyes, his whole life may be transformed. So, for the sake of transformation of human beings, enlightened Masters do anything. It is worth it. But the same things should not be done for any other reason. If it is done, people will get stuck and sucked into it instead of moving higher up.

Follow Me IN!

Q: I have heard many times that the Guru chooses his disciples. With you, I feel we have chosen each other. Am I wrong?

A: First of all, you don't exist as you think you do. You are constantly changing. Then, how can you choose me? You can never choose me. Only I can choose you.

Q: What is the reason for putting your face on pendants and T-shirts?

A: Ramana Maharshi, the great enlightened Master, used to sing hymns in his own name. He had compiled many songs on himself. Somebody asked him, 'Bhagwan, you are singing your own name. What is this?' He replied, 'Why are you reducing Ramana to this six-feet form? He is far more than this form.' Understand: I don't feel connected to the name Nithyananda or this six-feet form in any way. That is why I allow them to use it. You feel so connected to your name and form, and so you judge the whole thing from that perspective. That is where the problem starts.

One important thing: the form of enlightened Masters is like a *yantra* – a sacred tool meant for meditating. It is a form that Existence has chosen for taking birth as a human being. Also, it is a form devoid of any *samskaras* (engraved memories, that normal human beings struggle with). When you are constantly reminded of the form, or you are constantly seeing that form, you will unconsciously imbibe the superconscious energy behind it. That is why you will see, in India, the form of enlightened Masters are used liberally in pendants, calendars, etc.

Pranamaya Kosha

Q: How do I stop my rebirth?

A: Just get enlightened; that's all!

Q: How can we benefit from just temporary freedom from our identities, which we assume during this program? We have to anyway return to our obligations, to our duties and identities, as soon as we get back in our cars and go home.

A: When you do this for these few days, at least you will *know* that there is a possibility of getting rid of your identity; at least temporarily. When that possibility is inserted into your unconscious, then, you will never be afraid of living with your identity. As of now, you suffer because you know that living with an identity is like living in a jail. When you know that you have a key in your hand, the place where you stay in becomes a room. If you know how to get rid of your identity, even temporarily, the same jail will become a room. You don't have to get rid of it permanently. You don't have to get rid of it once and for all. You don't have to escape from your prison once and for all. Just have the key in your hand ... over! The same prison will become a home! You don't have to destroy the prison. You don't have to destroy the identity. Just have the key in your hand, that's all. Giving you the key, is what is happening through these few days.

Q: I know a lot of people who don't use their spiritual names legally. Why do you say that using the spiritual name legally is important?

A: When the spiritual name is given freely with no commitment, people ask for a name for themselves, one for their wife, one for their husband and what not! You see, choosing a spiritual name involves a lot of time and energy. I first categorize the people based on whether they are intellectually based, emotionally based, or they are a being level person. Then, I see the right path through which they will become enlightened. Then I give them their name. So, the name is given to them through the path in which they will become enlightened. Most people don't have respect for that process. That is why, these days, I tell them to be very clear whether they are willing to change it legally. Only then, I give them the name.

Q: Why do people wear the rudraksh mala? Does it have any spiritual significance?

A: Yes, there is a lot of spiritual significance to it. It can hold energy and radiate it for a long time. It is useful, especially when you fall into a low mood. It can support you with energy and the low curve can be dealt with in a beautiful way. Also, the number of times and the quality of the low curve can also be reduced by the *rudraksh mala*. It helps you, if it is from an energized being, from an enlightened being; not just from the shop. But of course, you can always wear it, meditate and request *Parashakti* (divine energy) to energize it.

Q: Please explain to us the significance of wearing the kumkum (vermillion) on the forehead, which you always do.

Pranamaya Kosha

A: It is done to awaken and energize the *ajna chakra*. I use it just to respect the tradition, and also, so that all our people will follow it. When they see me wearing it, they will follow! Then, whatever has to happen through that will happen for them. For me, it is not used to awaken the *ajna*! For enlightened beings, there is no such need. But if I wear it, people will follow, and their *ajna chakra* will be awakened. For that purpose, I wear it.

Q: *Also, what is the reason for giving vibhuti (holy ash)?*

A: *Vibhuti* is an energized powder. You can use it when you need healing for some part of your body. Or, if you have sleeplessness, apply a little of it on the forehead; you will sleep well. Whenever you need healing or energy, you will be supported by this energized powder. It doesn't mean that you will become addicted to it. Part of its job is also to elevate your consciousness, and therefore detach you from such addictions. The *vibhuti*, the holy ash that we give, is made out of our sacred banyan leaves. In the Bangalore ashram in India, we have a sacred banyan tree. The leaves that are shed from this tree are burned and processed, and *vibhuti* is created out of it. It is then energized and given to you. The tree itself is of a very intense energy. It has grown out of an enlightened Master's *samadhi* (place of his final resting). There is an enlightened Master's body under that tree. It means that the enlightened energy is there in that tree. That is why it heals. It radiates so much of energy. It is literally another form of an enlightened Master's body. It is actually equal to the relics of an enlightened Master's body.

Q: Why does one brood over the past?

A: Because you have nothing to achieve in the present.

Q: What is the cause of self pity?

A: Again, if you don't have anything much to do in the present, if you are too luxuriously placed, having too much of time to waste, then you do all these things. That's all, nothing more.

Q: Is the enlightenment state the same for all enlightened persons?

A: The experience itself is the same, no doubt. But the methods through which they reach enlightenment are different. After that, the state in which they stay is the same.

Q: How can we explain your philosophy to Krishna bhaktas (Krishna's devotees)?

A: Why do you want to explain to them? First, reach a state where you simply radiate me! Just radiate your *bhakti* (devotion to me). Live your devotion first. Then, you don't have to explain to anyone. Just by seeing you, they will be inspired!

Q: When we understand something on the intellectual level, when and how does it become realization?

A: Meditate, it will become.

Pranamaya Kosha

Q: There is a traditional saying in India: first Mata, then Pita, then Guru, then Deivam. Let me translate in English. It means: first Mother, then Father, then Master, then God. This is the traditional saying in India. This question asks: does this mean I have to fulfill the first three things to gain or attain God?

A: No. Understand: after your birth, until the age of seven, your mother will take care of you. She will be giving love, care, and all the basic things for you to grow. Then, she has to hand you over to your father. Between seven and fourteen years of age, your father will give you the basic education needed for life. He will give you education. Then, he has to hand you over to the Guru or Master! The Guru will teach you the science of enlightenment, between the age of fourteen and twenty-one, and then he has to hand you over to God. This is what this means.

Understand: the mother has to hand you over to the father. The father should hand you over to the Guru. The Guru should hand you over to God! Each one of them should hand you over to the next person and move out of your way! If they don't move out, they will be moved out! That's all. That is the way. That is what it means when it says, *Mata, Pita, Guru, Deivam*. The mother has to hand you over to the father and move out. The father has to hand you over to the Master and move out. The Master has to hand you over to God and move out. Even the Master who does not hand you over to God and move out, has to be moved out! This is what the saying means.

Q: Is it the same with female children also? Is it that female children are also handed over to their father at age seven, and then to the Master, and then to God?

A: Yes, yes, yes. In India, boys and girls are both treated in the same way when it comes to pure spirituality.

Q: So, does it mean that the father supervises the education of the daughter?

A: Yes. In India, the parents are supposed to be responsible for the education of their children. Not only education, they are responsible for their children's entire life. They have to create wealth and keep it for them! If your father or your parents don't keep wealth for you, nobody will respect them. Not only that, the children will question the parents, 'What have you done for me?' Even if the wealth accumulated by the parents is a little less, the children will ask, 'What have you done for me?'

That is the kind of social setup in India. Here, in the USA, it is totally different! Just see how Bill Gates is giving away so much money to charity. In India, you can't imagine this happening. The son will very well tell the father, 'What are you doing with the money? Get away. You are done with it. It is all mine now. Forget about charity!' The social setup is very different! Anyhow, this is the real meaning of *Mata, Pita, Guru, Deivam.*

Each one of them has to hand you over to the next in line. That is why I tell you in the healing initiation that you will be receiving tomorrow, there will be very clear instructions, 'You should not meditate on my form, the form of the Master.'

Pranamaya Kosha

Understand clearly: I am just like a window. You have to pass through me. You could use my help in the initial level, as a utility, but never as the goal. The Master's form is not the goal. The goal is the formless energy. Even this form, the form of the Master, must disappear! This form will also perish. This is not permanent. This form can never show you, or teach you to move towards the formlessness. One after the other, the steps have to happen, that's all.

Q: If I show love or acceptance to evil, won't that allow the evil to grow?

A: Don't bother about such things. You are not here to correct the whole world. Just correct yourself. Even if it grows, it is alright. Correcting mass evil is our responsibility. You don't have to bother about it. We will do our work, you do your work.

Q: You said that you may speak harshly to us to remove any evil in us. I don't know when I should smile at evil and when I should draw a line. For example, even though Durga Devi is a Goddess, she violently slays the demon. Should I also do that?

A: Please be very clear that you are not yet Durga Devi. You don't have to slay any demon. That is our responsibility. And understand: when you actually become Durga Devi, these questions won't rise in you at all! So relax.

Q: Sometimes, a child dies immediately after birth. Does he or she choose that? Why?

A: Yes. They choose it themselves. Why? You have to ask them. There are different reasons that each of them will have. You have to get a specific case for me and I will be able to tell you why.

Q: Can you say more about how to improve our eyesight?

A: In our Health and Wellness Program, we have a meditation for eyesight. Maybe you can try that. Even in the website, we have made it available. You can just download and practice it. Go to our website. All the main meditation techniques that we teach in our programs are available on the website. You can download and practise them directly.

Q: How do we relate with other disciples?

A: Understand, any undue relationship between disciple and disciple will only lead to problems, because both of you are in darkness. Any relationship between disciple and disciple will lead only to more darkness. There is a beautiful *Upanishad* verse on 'the blind leading the blind' - the blind relating with the blind.

Undue disciple-disciple relationship is such. It can be encouraged at only one point, and that is: when a disciple enriches your trust or devotion towards the Master, at that point alone, it can be tolerated, because at that point, the disciple

Pranamaya Kosha

who enriches your devotion towards the Master is no more a disciple; he is an embodiment of the Master's energy. Only through the touch of the Master, will he be able to enrich your love or trust towards the Master. Except in those moments, except in those few moments, the disciple-disciple relationship is very dangerous. I have seen people falling into a big hole because of disciple-disciple relationship.

In a city in Tamil Nadu, this incident actually happened. One organizer was very devoted, or at least projecting that he was very devoted. Sometimes, I allow these kinds of persons around me just because there is a possibility that they can transform. That is the reason. Not that they are really genuine. There is a possibility that, at one point, their ego can break, they can melt. Because of my presence being such an energetic and intense presence, they can break. So I allow them their ego. And one more thing: when I empower them, I empower them fully, and also protect them in front of others! Anyhow, coming back to this man, because of this, everybody was forced to come to me only through him. And this man, after some time, was able to command a group of people. I too encouraged him, because a good leader will be a good leader, as long as he is listening to the Master's words. It is good for everybody. Suddenly, at one point in time, I felt that his suggestions were stronger than my words. The rest of them also started behaving in a democratic fashion. I told them to relax. I told them that they did not vote and choose me as an enlightened Master. I told them, 'Fortunately, I did not stand in any election and get elected by you people as an enlightened Master. I just declared it myself. I declared that I am enlightened. And I am helping you. It is the individual relationship with me that is the base for the whole growth in you. Maybe for utility sake, disciples with the same attitude, gather in the same place to do some good work, some team work. That's all. That does not mean that you can do something foolish.' That is what I always tell these organizers. All organizers put together have not elected me. Understand: I am something more than all the organizers put together! Even if all the organizers together tomorrow appoint a disciple of mine as the Master, this kind of drama is not going to happen! It can never happen! So, the Master is something more than all these things put together. He is beyond these things. Understand that.

I always tell people: in spirituality, democracy is not going to work. Democracy is alright when it comes to administering a country or a political party, but not spirituality. And one more thing: relaxing at the feet of an intelligent, and compassionate leader is the best thing you can do. Understand: when you are with me, I am thinking for you! It is a great freedom for you that someone else is thinking for you! Do you understand what I am telling you? By thinking for yourself, you know the mess you can create. Just look back and you can see the whole thing. When you take the option of an intelligent and compassionate person thinking on your behalf, you are so blessed! Don't miss that opportunity. Somehow, in the so-called civilizations, the word 'surrender' is given a very wrong connotation. That is the problem. When you really feel that the leader is intelligent and compassionate, don't miss the opportunity. It is such a big opportunity. If somebody is building a home for you, will you miss it? If somebody is getting a car for you, will you miss it? In the same way, if somebody is getting you the best inner software, which is life itself, don't miss it!

Pranamaya Kosha

Q: For the past few years, I have started seeing flying particles in the air...

A: There must be some problem with your eyes. Go and get it checked with an eye doctor. Sometimes, you can see that if you look a little deeply in front of you in the air, you will see small air particles floating. It could be this that you are experiencing. It has nothing to do with spirituality.

Q: Thank you for your grace, instruction and time. I hope this question is not foolish.

I have been wondering if the connection I make with you and other enlightened beings carries over into my next life. And if you are not in human form, is the connection still there and how?

A: Understand. Even now I am not in human form. You may see the human form operating, but I am not in the human form. Just like how I handle this handkerchief, I am handling this body, that's all. It is a very beautiful and mystical thing. Alright, let me answer it. After that, we will enter into the process.

Nisargadatta Maharaj was a great enlightened Master who lived in India. He was being asked by a disciple: 'Maharaj...

('Maharaj' is the title by which they address evolved spiritual beings. Maharaj means 'king ,.. King of kings'. in India, Swamis are addressed as 'King of kings'. Even now, there is a protocol in the Indian constitution that, if a president or prime minister is received in any religious function,

Follow Me IN!

they are supposed to bow down to the religious leader present in that function. Till now, in democratic secular India, the constitution has retained this point. Even now, when the president or prime minister come to my program, the first thing they do is bow down. Of course, out of respect, I too bow down. The protocol is that they are supposed to bow down and I should take the seat first. Only then they will sit. Even now, in secular India, evolved spiritual persons are called 'Maharaj'.)

Anyway, the disciple asked, 'Maharaj, if you say that you don't have any karma (unfulfilled actions), what is the purpose of your taking birth? How does the body function?' The disciple is asking the enlightened Master this question. An enlightened Master does not have any karma (unfulfilled actions) from the past or future. Then how does his body function? For a body to function, you need some karma, some unfulfilled action, that causes it to move and fulfill it.

Maharaj replies, 'My body is not doing anything.' The disciple is shocked and asks, 'What are you saying? You are talking to me now. That is the karma. How do you then say, that you are not doing anything?'

Maharaj says beautifully, 'I am not talking to you.'

He is talking, and he says, 'I am not talking to you.'

It is very difficult to understand. Try to understand: I am sitting here. The truth is, I am just a wave in the ocean. When you want to listen, *because* you want to listen to something from me, *because* you want to experience something from me, this wave responds like a mirror. The Master says beautifully, 'I am not talking to you like you are talking to me. In you, there is

Pranamaya Kosha

somebody who is talking. In me there is only an echo which is responding.' Sometimes, when you go and stand in the high mountains and shout, you will feel that somebody else is shouting back. But there is nobody. In the same way, the constitution or the system is arranged in such a way that you hear a response coming in your own language. The beauty of the enlightened being is, the body is there without anybody occupying it, without anybody sitting inside it. You see me sitting here, but actually, you are sitting in front of an empty seat. That is the truth.

It is difficult to grasp. Maybe, if you yourself have some experience, or glimpse of the bodiless consciousness or the pure conscious energy, you will realize what is being told to you now. Maharaj makes a beautiful statement. 'I am not present as you think. I am not present as you are present. After both of us die, I will not be absent like you will be absent either.'

Understand: when both of us are in the body, I am not present in the body like you are. In the same way, when both of us disappear from planet Earth, I am not absent like you are. Right now, my absence has got a body. What I mean is, even though I have a body, I am actually absent! After death, my presence will not have a body, meaning, even though I may not have a body, I will be present!

I don't know how you will understand this. It may be too mystical for you. Alright, maybe the person who put the question can understand. Just try to relate with what I just said. My human form has nothing to do with the presence which you are feeling. Understand that clearly. That is why in the healer's initiation, before initiation, the Master takes an oath. I used to take the oath in the first level healing initiation, earlier. Now, I have shifted it to the advanced level healing initiation program, because these people don't take it sincerely in the first level. The oath that the Master takes is... he commits to the disciple, 'The energy which is working through this body promises you, for you to reach the same experience of the enlightenment energy, even if the energy leaves this body, even if the energy stops using this body...' I think you understand what I am saying. I am giving you the exact translation of the Sanskrit *mantra*... the energy which is working through this body commits to lead you to the same experience. Even if this energy stops using this body, even if I drop this body, the energy which is working through this body keeps its commitment to you.' This commitment may sometimes lead you to another live Master – a Master who is living in the body. It will see that you travel through and reach the destination - the truth, the experience.

It is a very strong commitment - much more and deeper than even marriage. Marriage happens in just one lifetime. And that too, nowadays, nobody cares much about it. The *mangal sutra* (sacred thread worn by married Indian women) is hanging on the shower pipe these days! In those days, Indian women used to wear the *mangalsutra* from the day they got married until the day their husband passed away. Actually, I don't feel that the *mangalsutra* should be imposed on them. In fact, it is usually the men who move around freely and have fun, so they are the ones who should wear the *mangalsutra*. Anyhow, besides the *mangalsutra*, even the depth of relationship has become very shallow these days. That is why I am saying, that the Master-disciple relationship cannot be equalised to marriage. Also,

Pranamaya Kosha

marriage is only in one birth. The Master-disciple relationship is for birth after birth, until you become enlightened; until you merge. That is the depth of the Master-disciple relationship.

The Master actually commits. Usually, in India, we do a *yagna* – a fire ritual - before any initiation. We invoke the fire, the divine energy in the fire, and before the fire, the Master takes the oath, 'Hereby, I promise this fire, which is the embodiment of the cosmic energy, that I commit, till you achieve the ultimate experience of enlightenment. The energy which is using this body, commits to take you, to lead you and be with you, to support you to that experience.' It is a very powerful commitment. The fire is supposed to be the cosmic energy.

Q: Swami, you said that whatever you talk is our echo. So, does it mean that you talk what we expect?

A: No, not what you expect, but what you *need*. That is where the consciousness comes in. I am not just a mountain. I am not just a plain mountain. There is the consciousness factor in me. Maybe, I am not just a *giri* - hill. I am Arunagiri – the sacred Arunachala Hill!

Q: Enlightened Masters will take care of the disciples until the disciples are done with their number of births. So, the enlightened Master in this birth will be in the body and take care. But how does he take care in the next birth if he does not take a body again?

A: He does not have to be in the body continuously to take care. He can guide you straightaway without the body also. He can straightaway connect and relate with you. Actually, intelligent people do not need me in the body. People who are already grown to a level of even 80 TPS, do not need me in the body. I can just send messages and they will be able to relate and grow. So, the work can be done without the body also.

But when the Master assumes the body, it is such a juicy *leela* (Divine Play!). It is so beautiful to see him in the body, to dance around him, to sing around him and do all the playful things! He assumes the body just to give juicy and beautiful moments as *leela* to people! Otherwise, enlightenment itself does not need a body.

You see, there are *panchakritya* or the five activities of God: creation, maintenance, destruction, putting people into *maya* (that is putting them in illusion), and liberation, giving you enlightenment. In these five activities, he does not have to take human form to do even one of these activities. All these five, he can do in the formless energy itself. He does not need the form for any of them. However, the fifth activity, that is giving enlightenment, can be done in a very joyful and playful manner. At that point, only for that reason, he may assume the human body and express the joyful energy!

See, the Master always comes down only for a group of people who have wished very deeply to stay around him, who are fortunate enough to stay around him and enjoy the drama. He is present maybe for a few thousand people, for a few thousand

Pranamaya Kosha

people who are going to be living around him and enjoying his innocent space. You can't even relate to that kind of life logically. It is just a spontaneous and joyful *leela*. For those few intelligent, or for those few innocent people, the Master assumes the form. When the water flows into the paddy, on its way, the weeds or the grass also enjoy a bit of it! The weeds also grow because of it. In the same way, I happen for a few people. When I move around for them, the others also enjoy. That's all. Otherwise, there is no need for the Master to take a human form. He is *asatyasangata* - anything which can't be done normally can be done just by his *satya sankalpa*; just by his mere true will.

Q: So, when an enlightened Master comes back to planet Earth, why does he have to go through the sadhana, penance again?

A: Because he starts from where he stopped!

Q: So we choose a form and a body based on what the previous karma is. Do we also choose our parents?

A: Yes. Parents, the place of birth, the time ... you decide everything.

Q: What about friends and relatives?

A: Friends are all societal. Even brothers and sisters are societal.

Follow Me IN!

Q: Wife?

A: Wife is surely societal!

Q: Swami, why would an enlightened being choose a new birth again after enlightenment?

A: Just out of compassion, also for Divine play! You see, it does not hurt an enlightened person to take a body. Nothing touches him. It is just a drama for him. It's like this: you guys are here now in the USA. After coming to this country, you have earned many dollars. Now, you can go back to your native village just to throw your weight around and have some fun, is it not? You go back to your village and show off, is it not? But it doesn't really touch you. You have gone beyond it. So, it is just a play for you. It is the same way for enlightened people when they come back to planet Earth!

Sometimes, you even take revenge on your young age associates whom you felt didn't respect you at the time when you were young! For me, there is no revenge in my system. I come and enjoy, that's all.

A small story:

Shiva was approached by the gods and Indra, (Indra is the leader of the gods) who told him that they were being tortured by three demons, and to please kill them. The demons were called Tripura Asuras.

Shiva said, 'Alright, let me take care. Don't bother. I will do something about it.'

Pranamaya Kosha

Then, all the gods came out and started talking amongst themselves, 'After all, Shiva is doing us a great favour, we should do something in return. What shall we do?' They decided, 'We will create a beautiful chariot for him, in which he can go and kill the demons.'

They created a chariot.

The four Vedas became the four wheels, the gods became the statues in the pasha (chariot). Finally, Yama, the Lord of Death himself, became the passa (the reins that control the horses). Brahma, the Lord of the gods, became the charioteer. Everything was ready.

Suddenly, Indra started thinking: all these things have been done by us. Then why do we need Shiva? We can, ourselves, destroy the demons also! We are enough to kill the demons if all of us put our power together. We have done this much. What is there in what is remaining? Shiva just blesses, that's all. He doesn't do anything anyway.

The moment he thought this, Shiva simply laughed. He said, 'Fool! I never asked you to do anything. You came to me and begged me to relieve you from those demons. Then your ego wanted to do something, so you built the chariot. Then finally your own ego is thinking that you are all needed for me to do my work!'

The story says that Shiva just opened his third eye and the tripura asuras, the three demons disappeared! They died. He just burnt them to ashes with his third eye.

So understand: sometimes, the disciples start thinking that they are needed for the Master, to do the work for his mission. Then, they are in trouble! So, that is the drama. A Master does not need anything to be done by anybody. His *satya sankalpa*, his mere will is enough to make the things happen. He plays his own drama and makes people feel connected to Him. He makes each one feel good. He makes them feel that they are also part of the whole drama . Otherwise, there is no reason why he should assume the human body. Blessed are those few who live around him and enjoy his very presence. This is like the story of the *Paramahamsa* – the Supreme Swan.

There is a beautiful story of the *Paramahamsa*:

Paramahamsa means the liberated Swan. The Paramahamsas will lay their eggs when they are flying. The egg will hatch in mid air and the tiny bird will emerge before seventy-five percent of the way down. The bird will grow wings and without touching the ground, it will just fly back into the air! It will always be in the air! It will never touch the ground.

You may ask then how Paramahamsa happens on planet Earth. You see, when he is flying, when the Paramahamsa is flying, the reflection falls on the lake or a tank or the ocean, or wherever. When the reflection falls, all the fish in the lake start thinking that some new fish has come amidst them! They think that some big fish has come. So, all the fish start jumping around the reflection. They say, 'Such a big fish has come. Such a graceful fish has come. See, how graceful this fish is!' The fish start jumping from one side to the other. Because of their own movements, there are ripples in the water and the reflection too appears to move. The fish think that the Paramahamsa is responding to their movements!

When the Swan flies over a lake in India, all the Indian fish gather and create a boundary around the reflection; they create an ashram!

Pranamaya Kosha

This is what happens wherever the Swan flies. Wherever the reflection falls, all the fish there gather together and create some monument. They collect small stones in that area and build a monument. Now, there may be several groups of fish from different places. Sometimes, these groups of fish start fighting. They say, 'Our monument is taller than yours!'

Understand one important thing: whether you jump towards the reflection and feel that it is compassionate, or you jump away from it, and blame it to be ugly and violent, it is all the play of only the fish. The Paramahamsa is not involved in any way in the whole drama! He is not even aware of the drama! If he closes his eyes, he will not even remember the names of the places where his ashrams exist, or the names of the planets where his work is going on, because he doesn't even know in how many thousands of places, and in how many thousands of ways his reflection is happening and dramas are going on.

Anyhow, that is the story of the Paramahamsa. Let us now start the process. Before entering into the process, for a few minutes, just sit and close your eyes; no *mantra*, no meditation, no prayer, no awareness, no technique. Just sit as you are. Even if you are restless, distressed, irritated, it's ok; just sit as you are.

CHAPTER 4

MANOMAYA KOSHA

- THE MENTAL LAYER

INTRODUCTION AND MEDITATION

The third layer is the *manomaya kosha* – the mental layer. It is the layer where your constant inner chatter goes on inside you. The inner chatter is nothing but the constant formation of words that happen in you, that don't bear any significance to anything. It is just a flow of words to do with irrelevant association of things, that's all. This constant flow is what we call 'worry'. If a person does not have a clean *manomaya kosha*, that is, if he is disturbed in the mind, sits as a leader, he can ruin the entire place where he is seated.

The *manomaya kosha* is the centre of all the five *koshas*. Not only is it in the middle as we know it, but even otherwise, this *manomaya kosha* can be called as a base of all the five *koshas*.

From *manomaya*, you can penetrate or work on all the other four *koshas*. Among the seven *chakras*, the *ajna chakra* is the *chakra raja* or the king of all *chakras*. In the seven layers, the *nirvanic* layer is considered to be the ultimate. In the same way, in the five *koshas*, the *manomaya kosha* is the ultimate one,

Manomaya Kosha

not even the *anandamaya kosha* or bliss layer. This is because, after the *manomaya kosha*, things are involuntary and not under your control. Whatever you can do, you can do it only up to the *manomaya kosha*.

We will work on this *manomaya* step by step. It will be a longer process than for the first two layers. The meditation process for the *manomaya kosha* itself is very simple. It is actually just humming. Intense humming itself will break the inner chatter.

When you hum, put your complete awareness on the humming. It helps you to silence the mind. Our inner chatter is created around the navel area. When we hum intensely, such that we feel the vibration of the humming right below our navel, we stop this process of continuous inner chatter. It is like shaking the whole thing up. So the humming should happen from below the navel.

Humming lets you feel your body as energy. The moment you start humming, you start feeling light, as if you are floating. You don't feel the heaviness in the body, because humming matches the vibrations of the mind with the vibrations of the body. Body and mind become harmonious. You start experiencing yourself as energy.

But you have to start at the *annamaya kosha* to enter into the *manomaya kosha*! It means that we have to start from square one. So now, you have to go through all the meditations you did earlier, because you slept last night. When I say you slept, I mean that you have fallen below the *vignanamaya kosha*, between the *vignanamaya* and *anandamaya koshas*. So now, you can't directly touch the *manomaya*. You have to go through the two layers, that is: the physical layer and the breath layer, and only then touch the mental layer. Let me explain why you need to do this. You see, the humming that you will do in the *manomaya kosha* meditation, as I said, will shake your inner chattering in the mental layer. Intense humming will completely clean your inner chattering. That is enough to work on your *manomaya kosha*. But now, if you directly do it, you won't be able to penetrate your *manomaya kosha* as deeply as we want to. In order to touch and penetrate it deeply, we have to work a little on the earlier two layers that are the *annamaya* and *pranamaya* layers also. Once you go deeply into these two layers, the humming will automatically do its work on the *manomaya kosha* directly.

So, start with the *annamaya*. Again, you will get into the animal body. Don't think that there is not much left inside you, after the earlier animal body meditation. There will be a lot inside you. Don't miss today's sessions. If you think there is nothing inside you, that there are no fear or lust *samskaras*, then come and sit here. This is the seat for you. You are enlightened!

Choose any one animal. You may choose the same animal as you chose the previous time or a different animal. Live in the same way, with the same fear and greed. Express the same feelings. Do not miss this time. Become that animal completely. Let the animal engrams heal intensely. Let them get cleansed. If you are not opening up and bringing out the engrams, you are lazy. At least be a buffalo in the animal body meditation!

We will go through the same process now. Next, we will do the *pranamaya kosha* meditation – that is bringing your awareness to all the five *pranic* flow processes. Then, we will do

Manomaya Kosha

the *manomaya kosha* technique - intense humming. When you hum, your mouth should be closed. Your whole body should vibrate with the humming.

I will guide you, and help you go through the whole process.

In the end, we will just sit for a few minutes for reprogramming, or entering into your *manomaya kosha* with an enlightened consciousness, for the *Upanishad* to happen!

Please make room for the zoo! Later, I will answer the remaining questions.

Meditation begins.. and ends.

'Just Sitting' again ...

Before entering into the next process, that is, the *vignanamaya kosha* or the visualization layer, just sit for a few minutes. No *mantra*, no meditation, no technique. Just sit for two to three minutes. Just close your eyes and sit. You may feel bored or restless. It is alright. Just sit.

(A few minutes pass)

Relax. You may open your eyes. We will go to the next process. Let me answer a few questions first.

Follow Me IN!

QUESTIONS AND ANSWERS

Q: During the animal meditation, I felt I was a wounded animal.

A: That is good. Actually, sometimes you will feel like an animal which is handicapped. It means that even those *karmas* are coming out. You might have left the body because of some accident. Do you understand what I am saying? You would have died in that animal body because of some accident or suffering. That is what is causing this feeling in you now.

Q: Two of the animals were wounded and the last time, before you stopped us, I found myself licking my wounds.

A: Ah, beautiful! Actually, the animals heal by licking! So it means that you have really gotten into that body. Beautiful, very nice! Somebody asked me what my role being here is. My role is pushing all of you; putting the whole logic to a silence and giving a strong instruction - for the whole group to fall into that experience. That is the role of the Master!

You saw in the morning: I spoke for one full hour. During that entire introduction time, I was putting the ego of the whole group down, I was putting the whole logic down, so that the space to trust the Master is created; so that more and more people can enter into the experience. The Master is a possibility; he is a promise, to open the door for more and more people.

One more thing: in earlier times, in the *Vedic* tradition, children got initiated through the *Gayatri mantra* as the first step towards spirituality. But before the *Gayatri* initiation, they would be made to do this animal meditation continuously for thirty to forty days. But nowadays, they do it only for three minutes! In three minutes what can you do? It has actually become like a ritual. In fact, most of the time these days, they don't even do this part. This is how the truth is lost in course of time. Actually, if you make children do these things, they will have a sharp and clear experience of the meditation, because they are not yet conditioned like us.

In India, in our *Gurukul* - which is a residential school for children in line with the *Vedic* tradition - and also in our *Little Anandas* program which is a fifteen day meditation program for kids, we make them do this animal meditation. Usually in India, kids attain physical maturity by 11 years of age. Before this happens, we make them go through this process so that they will be out of everything by the time they mature physically. This will cause them to be such pleasant human beings after maturity!

If the physical maturity happens after you have expelled the animal engrams, you will not only be a pleasant human being, you will also not fall too low or be too lust centered. The only animal that is lust centered throughout the year, twenty four hours of the day, is man. In reality, no other animal is filled with lust throughout the year and twenty four hours a day. Just a small suggestion is enough, and the body is ready. This is not the case with any other animal.

When you live with Nature, there is a period, there is a time, there is a mood, there is something called 'the body's ups and downs'. All these have to synchronize in order to indulge in lust. But because the mind has interfered in our system, these things have become immaterial. The moment the mind is ready, the body has to be ready, that's all. This is why we need to work out those animal engrams, before physical maturity happens.

In those days, before they gave the *Gayatri* initiation, they would make you undergo the animal meditation and during the *Gayatri*, they would tie a thread around the waist and give a *kopina* – a loincloth. Then, you would have a human existence earlier to physical maturity itself. You would be so graceful and feel fulfilled.

Those of you who wish to, may send your kids to the *Little Anandas program*. It happens all around the world.

If this meditation does not happen in them, once they become physically mature, they have to go through the same rut.

Q: In one of my animal meditation sessions, I was a vulture and I was eating something. Somebody came close to me, and I had to really fight not to whack them. In the second animal meditation, I felt like a silverback gorilla, and after that I stood up like a man. Then suddenly, I was an animal again.

A: Beautiful ma! It means you are done, *ma*. You have moved. You understand that you have moved. That is what is important.

Q: Swamiji, I was so afraid to be in the mental layers. I closed my eyes and felt like I was in hell. I just felt my fear and chanted a mantra.

A: Just go with that fear. No *mantra* will help to get rid of fear. Only facing the fear will work. Don't worry, I understood what you wish to convey.

Manomaya Kosha

Q: Here is a letter, It reads, 'Swamiji you could claim a miracle in my case. I have been suffering from joint pain for more than a year and everyday it was getting worse, having to take more than three medicines a day just to carry on. Yesterday, after the animal meditation, the pain has gone! This morning, the pain is not there; it is unbelievable to me and whoever knows me!'

A: Wonderful! Actually, these types of pain are also nothing but violence towards your own body. You carry a kind of violence in your body that expresses as pain.

Q: During the pranamaya kosha process, I felt as though I might inhale forever. I kept expanding. I would force myself to exhale because I would be scared of what might happen if I only kept inhaling!

A: Beautiful! The real process is happening.

Q: In yesterday's first process, I experienced anger and fear. I also experienced the confidence of a lion and the strength and confidence of a horse.

A: Beautiful! See, as I was telling you yesterday, the *vasanas* will leave you, but the power that they carried will stay with you. That is the power of that meditation. What you went through is really good for you.

Q: How do the techniques or processes purify our body of pesticides and other harmful chemicals?

A: I can say in a body that has toxins and other chemicals, the process of purification gets naturally delayed. What I mean is, it will take a few more times of meditation to achieve it. A few more times of the processes will be required because the body will not be very pure and receptive to receive the whole thing.

Q: The Meru mountain is often mentioned in scriptures. Does it actually exist in Angkor Vat?

A: No. The Meru is basically the Himalayas. Angkor Vat has got a huge temple, the world's biggest religious structure; a temple equivalent to the size of Manhattan, New York! It is a temple dedicated to Shiva, built by a great king called Mahendra Varma. It was actually built by six generations of kings. The structures were built near my native place in a place called Mahabalipuram. The structures were carved and transported through 2000 ships and assembled in Angkor Vat! They had to do this because there was no stone available for building it in Angkor Vat. They carved them, and used six hundred elephants to carry them! The temple is 96 sq. miles of built up area. It is completely made out of granite. Because there was no navigation and weather forecast information available at that time, only 50% of the material would reach Angkor Vot. They planned for everything, and for six generations they built the temple.

Q: Was he enlightened Swamiji?

A: No. He was simply inspired by enlightened Masters. In those days, the kings were always guided or inspired by enlightened Masters.

Q: Swamiji, is there a connection between Cambodia and Shiva?

A: The deity of Mahendra Varma's family was Shiva. So, they built the temple for Shiva. I don't know whether any special connection existed between the two.

Somebody is asking how enlightenment feels!

Just cool, that's all!

Q: Since divorce needs to be avoided, how about having partners without getting married?

A: If both of you agree, and your country agrees, there is no problem. It is up to you. But in *Vedic* tradition, we don't usually accept it. The reason is, we wish to emphasize again and again to you, that changing the outer woman or the outer man is not going to help in any way. It is like eating salt to quench your thirst. Your thirst will never be quenched.

Q: Can a female become an enlightened Master?

A: Why not? There are so many enlightened women - Maitri, Gargi etc. From time immemorial, we have had so many women enlightened Masters.

Q: I get nice fragrances during meditation and even during the prayer. What does this mean?

A: That's good. It means that your senses have become more alive and sensitive.

Q: I have had many deep experiences, but I am not yet living in full bliss. Do the experiences mean that I am flowering through my process?

A: Yes. You are on your way. You are allowing the process to happen.

Q: Did you get enlightened and then start living in absolute bliss, or did the bliss have to flower slowly?

A: You see: you can say, in a way, that my first experience happened at the age of 12. Then, it took 9 or 10 years to be established in that same state forever. So, it takes a little time.

Q: No matter how many questions I ask you, you refuse to acknowledge me, why?

A: Because you are asking the questions only for acknowledgement, not to know the answer. That is the reason.

Q: During *Ananda Darshan*, you give us tremendous energy, is it energy from heat or from the Kundalini that you get this energy. Is it there in you, all the time?

A: See, I am always an embodiment of energy. During *Ananda Darshan* time, I give it to you, that's all. Don't think that only during *Darshan* time, I get it. It is there in me always. During *Darshan* time, I make you feel connected to it, or make it available to you.

Manomaya Kosha

Q: One time you said that dreams are the mind's way of resolving and expressing any conflict within us. So, when you come to us in our dreams, what does it mean?

A: If you see me in your dream and if you are able to remember me in multicolor when you get up the next morning, then it is my *darshan*. If you are able to recall me as just black and white, then it is a just a thought, just a dream. That is the scale to know if it was a *darshan* or just a dream.

Darshan dreams or spiritual dreams will have a very strong impact on your inner space. You will be able to recollect it like a movie. But ordinary dreams, you will not be able to recollect like a movie. It will be like a vague and snowy television picture.

Q: How do I help others in my life move towards meditation?

A: Only by you moving, and radiating that quality.

Q: Is it best to avoid all toxins and harmful chemicals?

A: Yes, naturally. Naturally try to avoid all these things. Even things like preservatives, soft drinks etc., it is better to avoid as much as possible.

Q: What is the state of an individual after liberation? Is he going to be one with God or is he going to enjoy as a liberated soul?

A: He will be one with God. Before enlightenment, you will be away from it, and enjoying it, but after enlightenment, you will be *itself* and enjoying itself! You will be aware of yourself and just by being aware of yourself, you will be blissful also. That is the big difference between ordinary enjoyment and eternal bliss. See, in eternal bliss, you will become sugar and enjoy just being the sugar. In ordinary pleasure, you will be separate from the sugar and you will be enjoying it. With bliss, you will be the object itself and just by being it, you will be intensely enjoying it.

Q: Please explain how some of the poor people of India can be so happy also? We have everything here, and yet, are not happy.

A: You see: life should not be just a utility. You should have the freedom to waste your life also! Here, in the USA, society is such that it constantly puts so many consumerist ideas inside your head. It tells you: if you have money, you can have this, you can have that. It is an indirect peer pressure to make money. Constantly, it makes your life into a utility. Constantly, you sell your life, or lease your time to something or someone. That is the whole idea of working. What is the idea of working? If you are driven constantly by consumerist ideas, then you will lease your life to somebody. Constantly, those big fantasy houses are put inside your head. Life itself becomes a utility. That is why you are unhappy.

Now, even in India, in the metropolitan cities, this is how people are becoming. That is why they are also suffering. But in the villages, I have seen people who are still so innocent. Our neighbor at the ashram in India is an elderly lady. She was not even aware that she was a *crorepati* – millionaire in your language! She had a few acres of land which was worth crores of rupees. She was not even aware of that and she was struggling! Finally one day, she sold the land. After selling the land, she got a large amount of money, which she put in the bank. Then, she went to the person to whom she had sold the land and asked, 'Can I cut wood in your land? Can I cut trees in your land?' I laughed at her and asked her, 'Till yesterday, you did not have money. Now you have so much money. Why don't you use it?' Just the bank interest that comes out of her money is enough for her because she is living alone, by herself. But, she doesn't have that kind of attitude. You see, even if she has the money, that attitude of changing the lifestyle, changing the home, does not exist in her! That is the beauty! In India, people will have a lot of money, but they will still live in the same house. I have seen people living for three to four generations in one house.

My ancestral house where I was born and brought up, for a hundred and thirty year period, nobody fought over it, as to whose house it was. For a hundred and thirty years, neither my father nor his brothers, or grandfather or his brothers, have had any argument as to whose house it was. They did not bother to even check out in whose name the legal document was! Can you believe it? Anybody who belonged to that family felt it was their house, that's all! Only when they wanted to sell the house, did they start searching for the documents! This happens in many villages. Still, in many villages, nobody will bother about ownership of the parental homes. It will be like an open home. They don't change the house even if they acquire wealth. They just live in the same house.

As I was telling you, you should have freedom to waste your life a little bit, also. Then, you will enjoy life more. Then, you will experience life. It is not just a utility. You calculate your whole life based on money – the dollars that you make. You calculate: this month is worth this many dollars. For example, if you are making one million dollars in one year, naturally you will conclude that one year is worth one million dollars! If I tell you, 'Come to India, stay for one year and do meditation,' what will you think? You will think: no, no! One million dollars will go waste.' That is why I ask people, 'Since one year is equal to one million dollars, if someone will give you a hundred million dollars, will you give your life to them?' That is how you equate your life, am I right? You equate your life to utility matters. Then, receive the hundred million dollars and die!

Life just can't be equated to money. You should have a little freedom; you should have a social set-up where you are allowed to waste life also. A little fun is alright. When I say these things, it sometimes backfires, because people misinterpret it. In India, people feel that they have eternity in front of them. Because of the concept of rebirth, they never respect time. They keep thinking: if not today, tomorrow; if not tomorrow, next life. They have eternity in front of them, you see! That is the problem. That thought unconsciously stays in them and steers their day to day life.

Also, when I say these things, people ask me, 'Swamiji, are you not teaching laziness?' See ... there is nothing wrong in being lazy. But of course, I myself work hard. I work physically, continuously. Last night, after I went back from here, I attended to at least two to three hours of administrative work. Then, early morning, I got ready and came here. I do a lot of physical work because I feel like doing it. I never force myself. So, if you feel like being a little lazy, there is nothing wrong. You can't be lazy forever; you will go mad. So occasionally, just decide and be lazy, that's all.

Your body is made out of these three qualities – *rajas*, *tamas* and *sattwa*. *Rajas* means activeness, *tamas* means laziness, *sattwa* means being active but not restless, being peaceful.

Your system is made up of 33% *rajas* – active energy, 33% *tamas* – relaxing energy, 33% *sattwa* – active but peaceful. So you can't be lazy more than 33%. But you are never taught this. You are taught always that if you are not driven crazy, you will become lazy. Society never deals with the real truth. Even if you are not driven crazy, you will not become lazy more than 33%, because the *tamas* energy will be exhausted by then. After that, what will you do? How long will you go on sleeping? How long will you be lying down? So understand: you will automatically become active. But exhausting that 33% of your *tamas* completely, you are never allowed to do; society never allows you to exhaust your *tamas* fully.

And it allows you to believe that if once you rest, you will become lazy, once and for all… no! You will never become lazy once and for all. You should trust yourself. I tell people: sometimes, you should take a one month vacation and just eat and sleep. I mean it: you will exhaust the *tamas* if you do this! After that you will never feel like having so much of desire for laziness, or having so much of a desire to drop-out.

You suffer because you are suffocated with all these contradicting desires. Just once, you take a one month holiday or a vacation; don't do anything, just eat and sleep, and eat and sleep. Suddenly, you will see that you have exhausted the *tamas* and that the craving is not there at all. You see: experimenting with all these things is what I call *tapas*. Once you go through this one month period, any amount of work you do after that, you will feel that you are doing it because it is your freedom; it's your choice. So maybe, you can try it. I did it. I did it for nine years. I tried it for nine years. I would work only if I wanted to! I realized that life itself is such a big freedom after that!

Now, people who live around me, they know. At least twenty hours, I work per day. When I feel like sleeping, I sleep; when I feel like working, I work. My life and my routine have settled in such a way that I do not feel tired. In the last four and half years of my mission, I have not cancelled a single public program due to health reasons on my account. From my side, I have not cancelled a single public program. The reason for this, no desire for *tamas* exists.

There is no desire for *tamas* inside the system. The desire for *tamas* is lost. Your desire to be active, or passive - both are desires. When you are tired of being active, you start having fantasies and desires for renunciation. Renunciation based on *tamas* cannot be true renunciation. Many people come and tell me, 'Swamiji, I want to give up my job and come to India.' This weekend, Muni wanted to come. I said, 'No! It is based on *tamas*. You have to work, and only when I tell you, you can come.' Based on *tamas*, if you want to renounce, it will never help you. Exhaust *tamas*; maybe you can have a vacation for a month or two; just eat and sleep and exhaust *tamas*. After you exhaust the *tamas*, and after you exhaust the *rajas* also, *then* what you decide about renunciation of life, is the truth. I exhausted all the *rajas* and *tamas* in such a natural way, in *sattwa* actually.

Rajas will be exhausted if you achieve something which you never think you can achieve. When you do this, you are called

Manomaya Kosha

asaadhya sadhaka – achiever who has surpassed logic in achieving. Do something which you think you will never be able to do; then, your *rajas* will be exhausted. In the same way, *tamas* also... just rest to the extent that you can never imagine... eat and sleep, eat and sleep, eat and sleep. Don't even go to the next room for any reason. Don't even see television or read a magazine; don't indulge in any other entertainment. Just punish your body with rest. Ask your body: will you ask for rest, will you ask for rest? Your body should say: no, no, no, no, leave me! The body should be frightened by the very word 'rest'; then all your *tamas* will leave you.

These are things I call *tapas*; working on your *rajas* and *tamas* is what I call *tapas* or penance. Even this *Panchatapas* technique where you sit inside a fire circle and meditate for hours together is a technique to exhaust your *rajas* – making you do something which you never thought you will be able to do. Even fire walking that we do in India ... that is, walking on a bed of fire, which you might think is impossible, is done, to exhaust the *rajas* and *tamas*.

Q: What is the difference between meditation technique, no-technique and process? Can you explain one more time?

A: See, in the case of a technique, if you do it, it will work, but it will work only to the extent that you do it. In the case of the no-technique, it is again like a kind of a technique where you don't do anything, but you just relax into yourself. Again, it has to be done by *you* only. But the process is a mixture of everything, and not only that, you directly work with me in it. It can be done only with a Master. It's like using His presence in the optimum way. Just to do a technique, I am not needed; a teacher is enough. But for the process, an enlightened person is necessary. It's very intense and powerful, because of the presence of the enlightened person. It uses the presence of the enlightened being. That is why, the process is far more important than any technique. In techniques, nothing esoteric really happens, nothing mystical happens. But here, a lot of mystical things happen. Just by being a little sensitive, you will see so many things happening inside and outside.

Q: What is the meaning of God?

A: All that you can visualize and all that you can't visualize put together, *plus something more*, is God.

CHAPTER 5
VIGNANAMAYA KOSHA
- The Visualization Layer

Alright, let us now see the *vignanamaya kosha*, the fourth layer. This is the visualization layer.

Koshas and Boundaries

We need to understand the boundaries of all the *koshas*, the layers:

- The boundary of the *annamaya kosha* is your skin. Where your skin ends, the *annamaya kosha* ends.

- Second, the *pranamaya kosha*, is the distance upto which you can smell. If you can smell up to a certain distance of say ten feet or fifteen feet, *that* is your *pranamaya kosha*. Sometimes, it can even be up to thirty to forty feet, but not more than 100 feet. 100 feet will be the maximum. That is why people who have a strong sense of smell will be very sharp and intelligent. This layer is directly associated with intelligence. Such people will be very sharp in their decision making and clarity. But somehow, civilization has destroyed the sense of smell.

Vignanamaya Kosha

- The third layer, the *manomaya kosha*, is the mental layer. The boundary of the mental layer includes all the subjects which you can understand logically and which you are able to reproduce. That is the boundary of your *manomaya kosha*. If you are a doctor, all medical subjects come inside your *manomaya kosha*. Whatever you can understand logically and reproduce, whatever you are able to express, comes in the boundary of your *manomaya kosha*. Your feelings of love, hatred, depression, joy, jealousy or compassion are played out on this level. Ego and its natural characteristics and needs, are also manifested in the *manomaya kosha*. The *manomaya kosha* corresponds to your nervous system.

- The fourth or the *vignanamaya kosha* is whatever you can visualize or imagine. The people who live in visualization and imagination - like artists, poets, singers and painters live in this layer. They live a more satisfied, happy and deep life, when compared to the logicians. Lawyers and accountants may have money, but not joy or fulfillment.

A large firm which was doing scientific research, decided that it would experiment its medicines on lawyers, instead of rats. They gave three reasons for it. One: there are more number of lawyers than rats. Second: reducing the number of lawyers does more good to the country than reducing the number of rats. Third: there are some things that rats won't do for the sake of money!

RESIDE DEEPER WITHIN

Anyhow, artists, painters and poets, even though they live with less money, live with deep satisfaction, because their boundary is much bigger. For example, in a day, if you spend most of the time in the visualization layer, or the next layer that is the bliss layer, you will feel fulfilled. The time that you spend in the deepest layer, is what is going to give you the real fulfillment. Your fulfillment depends on that, not on the money which you make, or the car which you drive, or the house that you live in. All those things are not going to give you fulfillment.

For example, if you spend 10 hours in *annamaya kosha* and 10 hours in *pranamaya*, then you will have only two to three hours, in *manomaya*, and no time at all in *vignanamaya*! Then automatically, you feel that your life is dull and dead. That is why, if you have too much of entertainment in the *annamaya kosha*, you may feel good on and off, but depression will be the basic thread of civilization for you. Look at all the civilizations which have too much entertainment in the *annamaya kosha*. Depression will be the basic thread of that civilization. I am not condemning anyone. I am only telling you some simple truths.

The average time per day that a person spends sitting in front of the television, has gone up to seven hours now, in India. This is shocking. Actually, I didn't believe it when I read this report. I think in America, the average time is three and a half to four hours. One good thing is that, the majority of the population still does not have access to television in India. The crowd which does not have access to television is safe. But that number is also reducing drastically, because now the government is giving free television sets!

Awareness Is the Key

In the *Vedic* tradition, even entertainment was designed in such a way that you would be again and again pushed to the second or the third layer. What will such entertainment be? For

Vignanamaya Kosha

example, one such tradition is that you should go to the holy town of Tirupati, tonsure your head and pray to the Lord. But you also have people who go to the casino, give away everything, and come back!

Enjoying the probability is one of the important qualities of human beings. For example, if you play the slot machine, you may or may not win. Similarly, if you pray to Lord Venkateshwara in Tirupati, he may or may not give. That is the theory of probability. Our *Vedic* Masters knew that there are some basic instincts, which you can't kill in human beings. Enjoying probability is one such instinct. So, they diverted those energies in a proper way, and used them.

Enjoying probability is a basic instinct of human beings. Those few moments of anxiety, a certain kind of adrenaline release happens in the system. You enjoy that. Sometimes, you may feel frightened, but you enjoy it subconsciously. That is why you sit in all those terrific rides and roller coasters. During those sudden drops and wild rides, the adrenaline release happens in your system and it gives you a sort of a kick. So when you are in the anxiety that something may happen, or may not happen, that probability gives you a sort of a subtle kick. That is why you are sitting in front of a slot machine continuously. The same probability has been used by the enlightened Masters to put you into the third layer, the *manomaya kosha*. In the case of the slot machine, the same probability is used to retain you in the first layer, that is, the physical layer. But there, in Tirupati, you are just dropped into the third and deeper layer. At the end of the day, in Tirupati, the money collected goes back for social service. In the casinos around the world, the money goes back into the same business. And who is it who is controlling such a huge business? Who is

Follow Me IN!

getting empowered in the end? Just think! That is why I say, the right visualization can change the whole civilization. Just a few enlightened Masters changed the history of mankind. If you have to write the entire planet's history, all you have to write is the lives of ten enlightened persons. Their biography is the gist of the entire history of the planet Earth.

The more time you spend in the visualization layer, the deeper and more fulfilled your life will be. I am just throwing a few points, for you people to ponder over. Let me give an introduction to Tirupati for those of you who don't know. Tirupati is the richest spiritual center of the world. Per day, a hundred thousand people worship at the altar there. There is no city to support the entire infrastructure. People go to the top of the hill where the temple is located, and come down. Only very few people can be accommodated there. It is an amazing source of inspiration! Can you imagine a hundred thousand people gathering? During festivals, the gathering is around two million. Nobody prints invitations. Nobody is invited. Similarly, in the recent *Kumbha Mela*, another sacred Indian festival, about 91 million people assembled! There are no restaurants, no one sells food; all the 91 million are given free food! Selling food is a crime in that area. A hundred thousand tents are erected. Each spiritual organization takes up one tent and distributes free food. Their kitchens are open to all!

Spending more time and energy in the deeper layers will give you fulfillment. That is why artists, musicians, painters and poets feel so much more deeply fulfilled than the logicians, or the mathematicians. With logic, you stay in *manomaya*; with visualization, you come to *vignanamaya*. All your fantasies call you again and again back to yourself, back to the *samskaras*, just because of the joy you experienced in visualization. This is closest to the bliss layer. Because it is closest to the bliss layer, the smell of bliss will be there. Just to experience the smell, you again and again go back to the visualization layer. The fantasy itself does not have juice. I don't have to tell you this. You know for yourself that after cherishing the fantasy, for a few minutes what happens? You are bored. For example, if the joy comes from the sweet that you eat, then the joy should increase with the number of sweets, is it not? But that is not the way it is. After ten sweets, what happens? You feel repulsed by the sweet. It means that the joy is not from the sweet. There is some other source. The source, or the joy, is from the bliss layer, the fifth layer. Because the visualization layer is the nearest to the bliss layer, you tend to think that the source is there, and try to enter into the fantasies again and again.

MEDITATION
- VISUALIZATION OF EXPANSION

Now, we are supposed to go beyond this visualization also. How to go beyond the visualization? Because anything you do will be under your visualization. It's like going beyond your imagination. How can we? We *can*.

As I was telling you, anything which you can logically assimilate, is the boundary of your *manomaya kosha*. Anything which you can visualize, is your *vignanamaya kosha* boundary. For example, if you can visualize this room, it means that this has become your boundary. If you can visualize the entire hotel, it means that the hotel has become your boundary. If you can visualize the whole of Seattle, then the whole of Seattle has come inside your boundary. If you can visualize this whole country, the whole country has come inside your *vignanamaya kosha*

Follow Me IN!

boundary. If you can visualize this whole planet Earth, then the whole planet has come inside your boundary. If you can visualize the whole cosmos, the whole cosmos or the solar family comes into your visualization, or *vignanamaya kosha*. If you start expanding, and visualizing the whole cosmos, what will happen? At some point, your visualization has to break. It has to give way. Sometimes, it will give way even when you try to visualize this whole country. Sometimes, it will give way the moment you try to comprehend the entire planet. At one point, it has to give way.

I will guide you step by step. You will see that your visualization gives way. At least for a few moments, you will relax without visualization happening in your inner space. Let us see how it feels. Don't have the urge. If you have the urge, the very urge will stop the process. Just come along with me in a very relaxed way. When I say visualize Seattle, whatever you know about Seattle, visualize and feel it inside your skin. The traffic moving inside your skin. The whole thing is happening inside what you think as your boundary. Just expand your visualization step by step. Suddenly you will see that your visualization gives way to Existence itself!

Please close your eyes. Tie your eye bands. Sit in a very comfortable way. Do not lie down. Do not sleep.

Sit in a relaxed way. There should not be anything tight gripping your body. First, feel your boundary of the *annamaya kosha*, the physical layer. Feel yourself completely inside your skin. Feel yourself alive from head to toe. Go to your feet. Feel from inside that you are alive. You are alive inside your feet.

Feel yourself completely alive inside your skin: your head, your toes, your hands, your fingers; feel yourself alive everywhere.

Vignanamaya Kosha

Now, expand up to your *pranic* layer - about ten feet around you. Two or three people who are sitting around you are all inside you. Expand ten feet all around you. Feel that you are expanding up to your *pranic* layer, up to the space where you can feel the smell. Feel that the people who are sitting around you are all sitting inside you.

Now, just expand and fill this whole room. Feel that you are filling all the corners of this room. This whole room is inside you; including me, all of us are inside you. Everybody is sitting inside you. Just expand. These chairs, sofas, all the meditators, everyone sitting here, is inside you. Fill all four corners of this room. Fill this whole room. Expand.

Now, expand and fill this whole building. See very clearly: this whole building is inside your being. Expand and feel this whole building inside your body. What you think as your boundary, is now around the entire building.

Next, fill this whole street. See that the whole street is inside you. The traffic, the movements, everything is happening inside your body, inside your boundary. Fill it. Feel every inch of the street, feel every corner of the street to be inside of you.

Expand now, and fill this entire city. Whatever you know in the city, all the places that you know in the city, just bring all of them back to your memory, and see that everything is inside you. You are filling it. Every bit is filled by you. Every street, every road, every home, river, hill, everything... you are filling everything. Everything is inside you.

Now, expand further and fill all the corners of this country. Whatever you know about this country, bring it back to your visualization and see that you are filling all those spaces.

Follow Me IN!

Everything is inside you. All four corners of this country are inside your boundary. Feel that everything is inside you. All the movements, everything is inside you. You are filling everything.

Now, expand and just feel that this whole globe, the entire planet Earth is inside you. Whatever you know about this planet Earth, all the places that you have heard about or seen, wherever your memory can penetrate, expand to cover it. Let the whole thing be inside your inner space. Experience all the places inside your boundary, inside your skin, inside you. Expand. Let everything be inside you. Feel the oceans, mountains, rivers, cities, everything to be inside you. The whole globe is moving inside your inner space.

Expand further so that the whole solar family is inside you. The sun, moon, planet Earth, all the planets are moving inside you. Feel everything moving inside your head. Let everything be inside your head. See that you have expanded and the whole solar family is moving inside your head.

Now... expand further. Let the whole cosmos be inside you. The whole empty space, light covered by light, darkness covered by darkness, big bangs and black holes that are happening...whatever you know as the cosmos, expand and allow it to be inside you. Continue to expand. Feel the bliss in you. Feel the immense lightness in you. Feel the expanse of bliss in you.

You will start moving towards experiencing the *anandamaya kosha*. It is at the level of the *anandamaya kosha* that true yoga happens, where the union of mind, body and spirit takes place, where you are one with the cosmic energy; where the Self is alive and you have identified yourself with it!

Thank you.

CHAPTER 5

ANANDAMAYA KOSHA

- THE BLISS LAYER

The *anandamaya kosha* is not a sheath in the same sense as the other four *koshas*. It is the soul itself. It is a body of light. Experiencing this *kosha* is the whole purpose of this program. All the meditation we did till now are only cleansing processes for experiencing this *anandamaya kosha*.

WHAT THE MASTERS SAY

There have been many enlightened masters from time immemorial. Each of them experienced the Truth in a different way and each of them expressed it in a different way. Each of them had their own set of teachings. If one of them said vegetarian food was good, another would say that it was alright to have non-vegetarian food! Ramakrishna Paramahamsa ate fish and fish is considered vegetarian in Bengal, where he lived. One master would say that you should not enter into marital life in order to get enlightened while another master would say that it was alright to be married, you could still attain enlightenment. A third master would say that you could have as many wives as you wished to! So the teachings were always never convergent. But on one point, all the masters concurred. On one point they all converged and that was the statement: 'Man as such is bliss!' All the masters have this statement as their foundation and it is upon this statement, that the rest of their teachings are built. This is the underlying statement: Man's inherent nature is bliss.

OUR TWO PSEUDO IDENTITIES

To understand this single statement, we need to understand a few basic truths about ourselves: we carry two identities in us always. One, the identity which we project to the outer world, how we want the world to know us, how we want to present ourselves to the world, how we want the world to remember us. We call this word *ahankar*. Second is the identity which we believe we are, inside our heart. This is what we call *mamakar*. So we have two identities - the identity which we project to the outer world and the identity which we believe we are inside ourselves – the *ahankar* and the *mamakar*.

Our entire life is nothing but a fight between the *ahankar* and the *mamakar*. There is a constant struggle between the identity which we want to project to the outer world and the identity which we believe we are inside us.

When we think that the identity which we want to project to the outer world is reality, we become materialistic. We then spend our whole lives in trying to fulfill that identity, to make that identity into reality, to make that personality into reality. In our day-to-day life, we can see the kinds of people who want to make the outer world identity into reality.

The second group of people who start believing that the identity which they believe inside them is real, only become a kind of a religion. They become yogis, constantly chiseling themselves, constantly trying to develop themselves.

Understand: the identity which you project to the outer world will always be much more than what you are. It will always be something more than what you are. You will always be projecting something more than what is. And the identity which you believe as yourself in the inner world will always be lower than what you are. You will always be continuously condemning, criticizing and judging yourself. It will always be much lower than what you are.

The group which believes in the identity which it projects to the outer world, the *ahankar*, will become materialistic. The other group that believes in *mamakar*, the identity which it believes as itself, becomes a kind of religious group like yogis - continuously chiseling themselves, continuously working on themselves, continuously trying to develop themselves.

Very few people realize the truth that neither the identity which you project to the outer world is reality, nor the identity which you believe within as yourself is reality. People who realize that both are not reality, that both have no base, only they experience true liberation. Only they realize their true blissful state which is beyond both *ahankar* and *mamakar*. We call them *Paramahamsas*.

The Ancient Tradition Holds The Key

Spirituality, the traditional knowledge, the research and development which went on in India for the last ten thousand years in the inner science is capable of contributing something more than just the feel-good feeling that we are all trying to achieve. At least for the last ten thousand years in India, the research in the Inner Science has been going on. Millions of inner world scientists - great *rishis* and masters, and at least one crore Inner Science laboratories - our temples and places of *satsangs*, have worked in the inner world to achieve the Truth.

In India, we have more than one crore living ashrams and temples, where this science is continuously practiced by at least one million people. So this great technology, this great tradition has something much deeper and much more sacred to offer to us. It has something much more for us, if only we understand it. We can enrich our lives in the ultimate way with it. We can easily experience our *anandamaya kosha* with it.

UNDERSTANDING AND MOVING BEYOND

Understanding the *ahankar* is easy because it is something to do with the outer world. All you need to do is, come to a point where you yourself understand that you are struggling to maintain your *ahankar* or image with the outer world. That is enough, the job is done! The moment you realize you are unnecessarily struggling to maintain an image for the sake of the outer world, you will stop doing it! If you just sit for a few minutes and contemplate, 'I think what I am going to project is never going to be fulfilled or is never going to become reality', it is enough, the job is done. You can drop *ahankar*.

But if you start fighting with your *mamakar*, if you start chiseling your *mamakar*, if you start developing your *mamakar*, there is nobody to even tell you that you are caught in it because it is something happening within you. Trying to develop the identity which you show to the outer world, and trying to develop the identity which you believe as yourself, both will end only in deep suffering, because both have no base. Neither *ahankar* nor *mamakar* have a base. The moment you understand that these two don't have a base, that they do not have a hold over your inner space, then suddenly you will experience a great freedom, a great liberation, a deep restful awareness! This is the *anandamaya kosha*.

As J. Krishnamurthy calls it, it is called 'choiceless awareness'. That awareness is a real gift from our tradition, from our great *Vedantic* tradition. This awareness is the essence or the fruit of the research and development which went on in Inner Science for thousands of years.

Preparing To Un-clutch

So the first understanding is, both the identities which we carry don't have a base. They are not real. The second thing is, how to go beyond these two? It seems difficult because from the moment you come out of your sleep till the moment you fall into the dream state, these identities have a continuous hold over you. They have a say over you. They have an influence over your being. How to **un-clutch** or detach from them? This is the word that we will be using again and again. We will be using the word 'un-clutch' repeatedly for this *kosha*.

While driving a car, in order to change gears, you have to first press the clutch, come to neutral and then move to the next gear. In the same way, between any two thoughts there is silence, a neutral zone. When you move from one thought to the next, you will experience the neutral zone.

You have to disengage from the moving wheels before you change the gear, is it not? That is what is un-clutching. You have to disengage from the moving thoughts, from the moving identities. Whether it is from the first gear to the second gear, or from the

Anandamaya Kosha

second gear to the third gear, or any movement, you have to completely declutch or un-clutch from the movement first.

In the same way, any state you fall into, whether it is from the waking state to the dream state or from the dream state to the deep sleep state, any state that you move into within your inner space, you have to un-clutch first. You have to first come to that zero zone. You have to come to that neutral zone. You have to come to the centre space.

The centre space is continuously happening in you without your involvement. If you can experience that centre space with your awareness, suddenly you will experience what I call 'freedom'! What I mean when I say freedom is really freedom from these two main identities. You will experience a state beyond these two identities. Let me try to explain with a small example.

In North India, you might have seen in the forests how they hang a small stick between two trees in order to catch birds. The hunters use this trick to trap birds. The stick will hang between two trees in this fashion. You may wonder, how the bird will be caught by such a small thing. The bird will come and sit on one side of the twig. The moment it sits, because of its weight, the stick will turn over and become topsy-turvy, and the bird will hang upside down. The poor bird will not understand that if it lets go, it can simply fly! It will think that if it relaxes, it will fall and die, and so it will be continuously hanging on to it, for maybe even two to three hours. The hunter will come, slowly catch the bird, put it into the cage and go. Understand: just like this bird, we too have a great fear that the moment we let go of the 'I' and 'Mine', the *ahankar* and *mamakar*, we may become mentally imbalanced or we may not be able to run our day-to-day routine. This is the first fear. People always ask me, 'Swamiji, you ask us to relax from the two identities, the outer identity and the inner identity. If we relax from them, how will we be able to manage our daily routine? How can we even think? How we can live our lives?'

Understand very clearly that there is no reference or record of any bird having relaxed, falling and breaking its head. No! So if we let go, we will only fly. Just like the bird hanging onto the stick, we hold on tightly to our identity and continuously because our identity is our security. That is our security, whether in the outer world or in the inner world. That is our boundary; that is our security. The big problem is, when we hold onto it, we hold on only for security, but slowly, that boundary becomes practically like a boundary made for our bliss, our joy, our expression, our intense enjoyment.

The boundary which we create as a security, itself becomes a bondage or prison for our joy, of our very being. All that the bird needs is a little courage to let go. Maybe during the two or three seconds after it lets go, it might struggle to get its balance, it may experience a little chaos, a little difficulty. But after those few seconds, it will simply be in bliss, is it not? The courage to manage those two or three seconds is what I call *tapas* - penance. That is what is penance.

All we need to know is, the identity which we project to the outer world and the identity which we believe as ourselves, both have no base. Second: when you understand that both have no base, that they have no direct use to you in your life, that they do not directly contribute to your life, you can simply relax and play the game in a much better way without these two identities.

Anandamaya Kosha

The whole game which you are playing now, your whole life, your whole day-to-day routine, can be handled, managed and lived without these two identities coming into play or without these two identities remembered in your inner space as yourself. If this possibility is understood, then you have caught what I call the 'right listening' – *shravana*! You have finally rightly listened to my words! And if you are continuously contemplating and trying to live this newfound freedom, you have caught what I call *manana* – contemplation! You have finally started contemplating the great Truths. If you are established always in that freedom, we call it *nidhidhyasana* or living enlightenment! It means you have started living enlightenment.

Maybe in the young age, some fear and greed is needed to drive your life. But now, the maturity is in being driven by inspiration. That is what I feel is maturity. Even after becoming physically mature, if you have to be driven by fear and greed to run your day-to-day life, it is no good. But the problem is, we are never given the inspiration. We are never given the courage that we can live just by inspiration. We always think, 'Either there should be fear or greed, else I will become lazy.' This is not true.

Sometimes you can see, that for no reason you will radiate excitement and for no reason you radiate intelligence. Those few moments can be extended to become your whole life. That is what is experiencing the bliss body or *anandamaya kosha*.

THE UN-CLUTCH TECHNIQUE

- BREAKING THE PAIN AND JOY SHAFTS

Now, let us come to the un-clutching technique.

Follow Me IN!

If you observe your mind, you will see that thoughts are flowing continuously inside. And the thoughts are completely independent, illogical, unconnected, and irresponsible thoughts. These thoughts are not responsible for each other. They don't have a logical connection. They are completely independent and illogical; they are not connected.

Let me give you an example: you see a dog on the street. Immediately you remember some dog which you had as a pet or a dog of which you were frightened in your young age. Then, the memory of your young age comes to your mind. Suddenly, the thought of the teacher under whom you studied in your young age comes in. The dog which you saw on the street and the teacher whom you studied under have no logical connection!

You can take a paper and a pen and write down whatever goes on inside you, without editing anything, for just two minutes. Just transcribe whatever is going on in your mind. You will see that the thoughts flowing inside you are completely illogical, independent and irresponsible. Then what is it that connects them? What is it that connects them and gives you the kind of feeling that it is continuous and logical? The answer is 'your own mind'. For example, if you decide to connect all the suffering and depressing thoughts in your life and create an idea of a pain shaft, then you will conclude that your life itself is suffering. Then, because you have decided that your life is suffering, you will keep creating the pain shaft easily for yourself.

Very rarely when you are in a high mood, in an exciting mood, or when you are really in love with somebody, or some object, or with your life, do you feel that your whole life is a joy. And those moments you connect as joyful moments, and make a joy shaft.

Anandamaya Kosha

If you believe life is painful, you will create the pain shaft. If you believe life is joy, you will create the joy shaft. One important thing that you need to understand here: the depression which happened in you ten years ago, the depression which you experienced eight years ago, the depression which you experienced four years ago, and the depression which you experienced yesterday, are completely independent incidents. Our responses to independent incidents in our life are independent experiences, but when you connect all of them and see them together you say, 'My whole life is a depression.' This is the shaft that we must not create and this is the shaft we need to un-clutch from.

This pain shaft or joy shaft is created out of your belief. If you see the exact thoughts moving as they are inside your inner space, they are neither right nor wrong. They are, that's all. It is an existence, a reality, it is just flowing. But when you create an idea, when you want to restrict them, when you want to frame them for future reference, you either frame them as a pain shaft or a joy shaft. And the difficulty is you don't stop here.

The moment you identify your life as a pain shaft, you try to break it. If you identify your life as a joy shaft, you try to elongate it. Neither can you elongate nor break the shaft because the shaft does not exist in reality. It does not exist in reality. It is just imaginary. It is just your feeling. If it exists, you can break it. It does not exist. You are trying to break something which is not there! You are trying to continuously fight with something which is not there, either the joy shaft or the pain shaft. Again and again, we try to break the pain shaft; trying to break the pain shaft brings one more pain.

The words flowing, the thoughts flowing in our inner space, creating pain shafts or creating joy shafts is what I call *"Maya"*.

Follow Me IN!

In Sanskrit, we have a beautiful word *"Maya"*, that which is not there, but gives the suffering as if it is there. Even if it is not there, if it gives the suffering as if it were there, then it is called *'Maya'*. It is not there, but it gives the suffering or the impression as if it is there. The thoughts which are arising in your being are the root cause of your suffering.

Let me give you a simple technique of unclutching. Please understand, it is a simple technique of unclutching. What do I mean by the word 'unclutching'? When you sit, there will naturally be some thoughts. When thoughts arise, usually your mind will tell you to connect it, identify it with some past pain or joy. Or it will classify them as something related to worry, or there is nothing, simply thoughts flowing. It will try to connect or classify. It will try to clutch with some of your past experiences and identify them.

Now just for few moments, try this experiment. When any thought comes, do not clutch it with your past experience, do not clutch it with your past suffering or joy. When words come out of your being, instead of giving meaning to them, just see the source of the sound. You see, sounds are rising from your inner space and the moment you give them meaning, you become materialistic.

And understand: thoughts arise only one after another in you. For one thought to arise, the previous thought should have died, else there is no way that this thought could have surfaced. If you are sitting now, and you suddenly decide to stand up, then the thought that you have to sit should have left you at that very moment, otherwise you cannot stand up, am I right?

If you apply this to every single thought of yours, you will realize that every thought simply rises and dies and the next thought

Anandamaya Kosha

rises. But what do we do? We gather all the thoughts that have died as well, and make our shafts and suffer. If you stop connecting the thoughts, your mind will disappear and you will be in pure thoughtless awareness or bliss body. If you catch this technique of un-clutching from your thoughts, you can catch the zone of thoughtless awareness or bliss!

MEDITATION

NITHYA DHYAAN - LIFE BLISS MEDITATION

This meditation expels the engraved memories in us that cause us to create the pain or joy shafts. It creates a harmonizing and balancing energy in us and keeps us in an energized and blissful state. This meditation is the essence of all my years of research in the Inner Science till date.

Before entering into the *Nithya Dhyaan* meditation, you need to know that there are seven vital energy centers in our body that are responsible for our emotional and physical health. When we learn to handle our emotions in the best possible way, we keep these *chakras* open, and they in turn keep us energized. If we get caught in our emotions of the past or the future, these energy centers get closed and we fall into physical or mental illness. The base energy center, the *muladhara chakra* is associated with the emotion that is lust or desire, the *swadhistana chakra* is associated with the fear emotion, the *manipuraka* with worry, the *anahata* with attention-need, the *vishuddhi* with jealousy, the *ajna* with ego and the *sahasrara*

with discontent. When we understand our negative emotions and rectify them, these *chakras* open up and radiate energy for us. The third step of this meditation is to do with these 7 *chakras*.

Step 1: Sit in *vajrasana* (if not possible, sit cross-legged or on a chair) with hands on your hips. Close your eyes and breathe chaotically for 7 minutes.

Step 2: Continue to sit in *vajrasana* (if not possible, sit cross-legged or on a chair). Form '*chin mudra*' with your fingers (form a circle with thumb and forefinger of both hands, palm upwards), and placing your hands on your knees, hum intensely for 7 minutes. Keep your lips together while humming. Hum as loudly, as deeply from your navel center and as lengthily as possible.

Step 3: You may now sit cross-legged on the floor if you wish to or continue to sit in *vajrasana* and for 7 minutes, take your awareness from the *muladhara chakra* to the *sahasrara chakra*. Dwell on each *chakra* for a minute with deep awareness. Visualize that there is nothing in this world except that *chakra* on which you are meditating.

    a.   Take your awareness to the *muladhara chakra*.
           Your *muladhara* is pure
           Your *muladhara* is filled with energy
           Your *muladhara* is overflowing with bliss
           Your *muladhara* is radiating *nithyananda*
           (*After 1 minute*)

Anandamaya Kosha

b. Take your awareness to the *swadhistana chakra* which is two inches above the *muladhara*.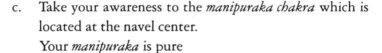
Your *swadhistana* is pure
Your *swadhishtana* is filled with energy
Your *swadhistana* is overflowing with bliss
Your *swadhistana* is radiating *nithyananda*
(After 1 minute)

c. Take your awareness to the *manipuraka chakra* which is located at the navel center.
Your *manipuraka* is pure
Your *manipuraka* is filled with energy
Your *manipuraka* is overflowing with bliss
Your *manipuraka* is radiating *nithyananda*
(After 1 minute)

d. Take your awareness to the *anahata chakra* which is located at the heart center.
Your *anahata* is pure
Your *anahata* is filled with energy
Your *anahata* is overflowing with bliss
Your *anahata* is radiating *nithyananda*
(After 1 minute)

e. Take your awareness to the *vishuddhi chakra* which is located at the throat center.
Your *vishuddhi* is pure
Your *vishuddhi* is filled with energy

Your *vishuddhi* is overflowing with bliss
Your *vishuddhi* is radiating *nithyananda*
(After 1 minute)

f. Take your awareness to the *ajna chakra* which is located in the region between your eyebrows.
Your *ajna* is pure
Your *ajna* is filled with energy
Your *ajna* is overflowing with bliss
Your *ajna* is radiating *nithyananda*
(After 1 minute)

g. Take your awareness to the *sahasrara chakra* which is located in the crown center.
Your *sahasrara* is pure
Your *sahasrara* is filled with energy
Your *sahasrara* is overflowing with bliss
Your *sahasrara* is radiating *nithyananda*
(After 1 minute)

Step 4: For 7 minutes just be un-clutched in silence.

Step 5: For the last few minutes, listen to the Guru Puja *mantras* being played. This is an offering of gratitude to the lineage of enlightened masters for the Inner Science research done by them for over thousands of years. (You may refer to the **Do Guru Puja Yourself** book for a detailed explanation of the Guru Puja *mantras*).

Appendix

Appendix

Follow Me IN!

About Nithyananda

It was under the glow of the spiritual magnet Arunachala in the energy center of Tiruvannamalai in South India, that Nithyananda was born - as Rajasekharan, to Arunachalam and Lokanayaki on 1 January, 1978. The family astrologer predicted that he would be a king amongst holy men.

At the age of 3, Nithyananda was associated with Yogiraj Raghupati Maharaj, a yoga guru who took him through rigorous training and prepared his body, with apparent foresight into the energy explosion that was going to happen in the young body. From the age of 5, Nithyananda took to deity worship with great passion. He showed profound commitment to the rituals he practiced with the deities. Just a few years later, he came in touch with Mataji Kuppammal, a deeply pious lady who initiated him into *Vedanta* and *Tantra* and started his scriptural learning at that young age. Encountering many mystics from the town of Tiruvannamalai, he received esoteric teachings from them.

At the age of 12, he had his first deep spiritual experience: while sitting on a rock on the Arunachala hillock, he suddenly had a 360 degree panoramic vision, and experienced becoming one with everything around

The earliest picture of Nithyananda in meditation taken when he was 10 years old

Appendix

him. This experience further inspired him to forge ahead in his journey inwards.

Academics at school and polytechnic came naturally for Nithyananda. With only the attention he gave in classes, he passed all his grades with distinction. He obtained a diploma degree in Mechanical Engineering from a leading private Polytechnic in Tamilnadu.

Nithyananda meditating in Arunachala

At the age of 17, he left home driven by the irresistible urge to jump into the real life that he was seeking. He wandered through the length and breadth of India studying Eastern metaphysical sciences and meeting many masters and mystics. He visited many great shrines, ranging from the Himalayas in the North, to Kanyakumari in the South, from Dwaraka in the West to Ganga Sagar in the East. After enduring intense meditation and other austerities, he attained eternal inner bliss...the state of *nithyananda*. At the age of 22, Rajasekharan became Paramahamsa Nithyananda.

Guided by Divine Vision, on Jan. 2003, Parahamamsa set up his

Flagging off construction at the mission site, Bangalore

Follow Me IN!

mission headquarters in Bangalore, India, in the land of mystical and sacred banyan tree.

Today, Nithyananda is an inspiring personality for millions of people worldwide. From his experience of the Truth he has formulated and makes available the Technology of Bliss to every individual. His methods empower us to be physically and mentally fit, with sound spiritual strength in both the inner and outer worlds. Millions of people around the world have experienced radical transformation through his techniques in short periods of time.

Nithyananda gives the tools to live a creative and productive life, guided by intuition and intelligence, rather than by intellect or instinct. He shows the way to excellence in the outer world and radiance in the inner world at the same time. His programs guide one to fall into the natural space known as meditation.

He says, 'Meditation is the master key that can bring success in the material world, and deep fulfillment in your space within.' His powerful techniques and processes that comprise the meditative programs help the flowering and expansive explosion of the individual consciousness.

Nithyananda cooperates with scientists and researchers the world over, to record mystic phenomena through scientific data. He intrigues the world of medical science with results from his own neurological system. From the astounding observations, scientists feel that the potential for altering the rates and progression of diseases like heart ailments, cancer, arthritis, alcoholism, etc. are beginning to look achievable.

Appendix

About Nithyananda Mission

Sacred banyan tree, Bidadi ashram, India

Nithyananda Mission is Nithyananda's worldwide movement for meditation and transformation. Established in the year 2003, the Mission continues to transform humanity through transformation of the individual.

Nithyananda Mission ashrams and centers worldwide serve as spiritual laboratories where inner growth is profound and outer growth is a natural consequence. These academies are envisioned to be a place and space to explore and explode, through a host of activities, from meditation to science.

Hyderabad ashram, India

They offer Quantum Spirituality, where material and spiritual worlds merge and create blissful living; where creative intelligence stems from deep consciousness. **Nithyananda Dhyanapeetam** is the spiritual wing that takes care of the spiritual activities of the mission.

Los Angeles Temple, USA

Follow Me IN!

Seattle Temple, USA

Many projects are in development at the various academies worldwide; and new academies are being established to provide services in varied fields to humanity at large.

A diverse range of meditation programs and social services are offered worldwide through the Foundation. Free energy healing through the Nithya Spiritual Healing system, free education to youth, encouragement to art and culture, satsangs (spiritual circles), personality development programs, corporate programs, free medical camps and eye surgeries, free meals at all ashrams worldwide, a one-year free residential spiritual training program in India called the Life Bliss Technology, an in-house *Gurukul* system of learning for children, and many more services are offered around the world.

Salem ashram, India

Columbus ashram, Ohio, USA

Appendix

Ananda Sevaks of the Nithya Dheera Seva Sena (NDSS) volunteer force comprising growing numbers of dedicated volunteers around the world, support the mission with great enthusiasm.

Offerings from Life Bliss Foundation (LBF)

Life Bliss Foundation is the teachings wing of Nithyananda Mission that offers specialized meditation programs worldwide, to benefit millions of people at the levels of body, mind and spirit. A few of them are listed below:

Life Bliss Program Level 1 - Ananda Spurana Program (LBP Level 1 - ASP)

- Energize yourself

A *chakra* workout program that relaxes and energizes the seven major *chakras* in your system. It gives clear intellectual and experiential understanding of your various emotions - greed, fear, worry, attention need, stress, jealousy, ego, discontentment etc. It is designed to create a spiritual effect at the physical level. It is a guaranteed life solution to experience the reality of your own bliss. It is a highly effective workshop, testified by millions of people around the globe.

Life Bliss Program Level 2 - Nithyananda Spurana Program (LBP Level 2 - NSP)

- Death demystified!

A program that unleashes the art of living by demystifying the concept of death. If you know the process and purpose of death, you will live your life in an entirely different way! It creates the space to detach from ingrained and unconscious emotions like guilt, pleasure and pain, all of which stem from the ultimate fear of death. It is a gateway to a new life driven by natural intelligence and spontaneous enthusiasm.

Follow Me IN!

Life Bliss Program Level 3 - Atma Spurana Program (LBP Level 3 - ATSP)

- Connect with your Self!

This is a breakthrough program that analyzes clearly the workings of the mind and shows you experientially how to be the master of the mind rather than let it rule over you. It involves the whole tremendous intellectual understanding coupled with novel meditations to produce instant experiential understanding.

Life Bliss Technology (LBT)

Life Bliss Technology (LBT) is a one-year residential program for youth aged between 18 and 30 years of age, on practical life skills. With its roots in the Eastern system of Vedic education, this program is designed to empower modern youth with good physical, mental and emotional health. By nurturing creative intelligence and spontaneity, and imparting vocational skills, it creates economically and spiritually self-sufficient youth.

Above all, it offers a lifetime opportunity to live and learn under the tutelage of an enlightened Master!

Nithya Spiritual Healing

- Healing through Cosmic energy

A unique and powerful means of healing through the Cosmic energy, this is a meditation for the healer and a means to get healed for the recipient of the healing. Nithyananda continues to initiate thousands of Nithya Spiritual Healers worldwide into this scientific and time-tested healing technique which has healed millions of people of ailments ranging from migraine to cancer.

Appendix

Nithya Dhyaan
- Life Bliss Meditation

Become one among the millions who walk on planet Earth – Un-clutched! Register online and get initiated.

Nithya Dhyaan is a powerful everyday meditation prescribed by Nithyananda to humanity at large. It is a formula or a technique, which is holistic and complete. It works on the entire being to transform it and make it ready for the ultimate experience of enlightenment to dawn. Each segment of this technique complements the remaining segments to help raise the individual consciousness. It trains you to un-clutch from your mind and live a blissful life. It is the meditation for Eternal Bliss.

If you wish to be initiated into Nithya Dhyaan, you may visit http://www.dhyanapeetam.org and register online. You will receive through mail, a *mala*, bracelet, a spiritual name given by Nithyananda for your own spiritual growth (optional), Nithya Dhyaan Meditation CD and Nithya Dhyaan booklet in a language of your choice, personally signed by Nithyananda (mention your choice in the comment column).

Nithyananda says, 'My advent on planet Earth is to create a new cycle of individual consciousness causing Collective Consciousness to enter the Superconscious zone.'

To achieve this,

Hundred thousand people will be initiated to live as *Jeevan Muktas* – liberated beings experiencing 'living enlightenment', and 1 billion people will be initiated into Nithya Dhyaan – Life Bliss Meditation – designed to cause a shift in the individual consciousness on planet Earth.

Follow Me IN!

Contact us

USA:

Los Angeles
Los Angeles Vedic Temple
9720 Central Avenue, Montclair,
CA 91763
USA
Ph.: 1-909-625-1400
Email: programs@lifebliss.org
URL: www.lifebliss.org

Florida
International Vedic Hindu University
113 N. Econlockhatchee Trail, Orlando
Florida, 32825
Ph.: 626-272-4043

New York
Queens Vedic Temple
129-10 Liberty Avenue, Richmond Hill,
Queens NY 11420
Ph.: 718-296-1995

Ohio
Ohio Ashram
820 Pollock Rd,
Delaware, Ohio
Ph: 740-362-2046

Appendix

Oklahoma
Oklahoma City Vedic Temple
3048 N. Grand Blvd.
Oklahoma city
OK 73107
Ph.: 405-833-6107

Missouri
St Louis Vedic Temple
8201 Nithyananda Ave,
House Springs, MO 63051
Ph.: 314-849-6760

Washington
Seattle Vedic Temple
2877 152nd Ave Ne building 13
Redmond Washington 98052
Ph.: 425-591-1010

Phoenix
Phoenix Temple
6605 South 39th Ave,
Phoenix, AZ 85041
Ph.: 480 388 2490
Email: vedictemplephx@yahoo.com

MALAYSIA

Malaysia Ashram
No. 14, Jalan Desa,
Gombak, S Taman,
Desa Gombak, Kuala Lumpur, Malaysia
Email: nirantaraananda@gmail.com
Phone: + 603 337 10980/+ 601 223 50657/ + 601 788 61644

Follow Me IN!

Klang Ashram
No 62, Jalan Serempang Dua,
Off Jalan Sungai Betek,
Taman Betek Indah,
41400 Klang, Malaysia

INDIA

Bangalore, Karnataka
(Spiritual headquarters. Vedic Temple located here)
Nithyananda Dhyanapeetam
Nithyanandapuri
Kallugopahalli, Mysore Road, Bidadi
Bangalore - 562 109
Karnataka
Ph.: +91+80 27202801 / 92430 48957
Telefax:: 27202084
Email: mail@nithyananda.org
URL:www.nithyananda.org

Varanasi, Uttar Pradesh
NithyanandaDhyanapeetam
Leelaghar Bldg,
Manikarnika Ghat,
Varanasi
Ph.: 99184 01718

Hosur, Tamil Nadu
Nithyananda Dhyanapeetam
Nithyanandapuri,
Kanuka Estate, Nallur post,
Hosur - 635 109
Krishnagiri District,
Tamilnadu
Ph.: 99947 77898 / 99443 21809

Appendix

Hyderabad, Andhra Pradesh
Sri Anandeshwari Temple,
Nithyananda Giri,
Pashambanda Sathamrai Village
Shamshabad Mandal
Rangareddy District - 501 218
Andhra Pradesh
Ph.: 91 +84132 60311 / 60044
Mob.: 98665 00350 / 93964 82358

Salem, Tamil Nadu
Nithyananda Dhyanapeetam
Nithyanandapuri
102, Azhagapurampudur
Salem – 636 016
Tamilnadu
Ph.: +91 94433 64644 / 94432 35262
(Behind Sharada College)

Namakkal, Tamil Nadu
Nithyananda Dhyanapeetam
Nithyanandapuri,
2/200, Tirumangkuruchi Post,
Namakkal – 637003
Tamilnadu, INDIA
Ph.: +91 +94433 88437

Tiruvannamalai, Tamil Nadu
Nithyananda Dhyanapeetam
Nithyanandapuri,
Opposite Rajarajeswari Temple
Girivalam path
Tiruvannamalai
Ph.: 94449 91089 / 94432 33789

Follow Me IN!

Pattanam, Tamil Nadu
Nithyananda Dhyanapeetam
Nithyanandapuri, Puthupatti road,
Pattanam
Rasipuram (Taluk) - 605602
Namakkal disrict
Ph.: 04287 222842

Rajapalayam, Tamilnadu
Nithyananda Dhyanapeetam
Nithyanandapuri,
Kothainachiarpuram,
Rajapalayam,
Virudhunagar District
Ph.: 04563 260002 / 94426 23768

Pondicherry, Tamilnadu
Nithyananda Dhyanapeetam
Nithyanandapuri,
Embalam to Villianoor main road,
Embalam post,
Pondicherry - 605 106
Ph.: 94420 36037 / 97876 67604

Poompuhar Aadeenam, Tamilnadu
Shivarajayoga Mutt
Opposite Poompuhar College
Melayur Post
Seerkaali Taluk
Nagai District - 609 107

For a list of centres worldwide, visit www.nithyananda.org

Appendix

Suggested for further reading

- Guaranteed Solutions for lust, fear, worry ....
- Nithyananda Vol. 1 (The first volume of a biographical account of Nithyananda)
- Life Bliss Program Level 2 - Nithyananda Spurana Program
- Follow me IN! (Life Bliss Program Level 3 - Atma Spurana Program)
- You can Heal (Nithya Spiritual Healing)
- Meditation is for you
- Bliss is the path and the goal
- The only way out is IN
- Rising in love with the Master
- Bhagavad Gita series
- Uncommon answers to common questions
- Open the door...Let the breeze in!
- Nithya Yoga - The Ultimate Practice for Body, Mind & Being

To purchase books and other items, visit www.lifeblissgalleria.com or contact us.

Visit http://www.youtube.com/lifeblissfoundation to view over 400 FREE video discourses of Nithyananda.